CW01044056

Lilac-breasted

kruger
birds

Philip van den Berg

HPH Publishing

Malachite Kingfisher

CONTENTS

INTRODUCTION

Southern Africa has a great variety of different climates, biomes, vegetation types and general habitats, which in turn give rise to an amazing richness of birdlife. The Greater Kruger is situated in the savanna biome and more than half of all the bird species in southern Africa occur here.

Birding is becoming more popular than ever. Use this book to make it easier for you to become familiar with the birds that are usually or most often seen on game drives in the Greater Kruger area.

Kruger Birds is a comprehensive guidebook that covers 447 Greater Kruger species. The main body focuses on birds you may see on a regular game drive or are striking in appearance and behaviour. The grouping here is unconventional and is based on shared habitat. Where further subdivisions are necessary, other factors are used to make more distinctions. Bear in mind that the groupings into habitats are not mutually exclusive and many birds will naturally occur in two or even three of the habitats. These broad divisions will help to make quick and easy sense of what can be a bewildering range of birds. The index section is a convenient 'quick find' section based on related species. The smaller pictures are grouped according to families and is the conventional way of presenting bird species. The numbers next to the images refer to page numbers in the first section of the book. **Note that some species listed in the index do not feature in the first part of the book.**

The first section starts with birds of prey. The water habitat and its attendant birds is a good place to start for any novice because of its clear boundaries. Ground-living birds seem to be everywhere and are easy to recognise. A few grassland birds are included under the heading of ground-living birds. Many grassland birds are difficult to identify and have not been included in this section. The vast majority of birds keep to bushes and trees and are more difficult to identify. Some of the tree-living birds also get their food on the ground but

Western Cattle Egret

return to perch on trees, others get food from leaves, flowers, fruits and seeds. Others use trees as a vantage point for hunting insects and other invertebrates while many utilise food they get on and in the bark of trees.

A few tips for birders:

- Approach birds with the minimum disturbance and sit quietly, watching with your binoculars.
- Avoid noise and sudden movements.
- Birds are most active between dawn and 11:00 and again from 16:00 until nightfall.
- Birds are colour-conscious, and their vision is up to two and a half times more powerful than ours.

THE BIG SIX

Avid birders and conservationists often group the most sought-after birds in Kruger as the Big Six. All of them are magnificent in appearance and in behaviour. Kruger and other conservation areas are a safe haven but even here their survival is affected by human activities in areas surrounding the park.

Pel's Fishing Owl

Martial Eagle

Kori Bustard

Lappet-faced Vulture

Southern Ground Hornbill

Saddle-billed Stork

9

BIRDS OF PREY

Bateleur

BIRDS OF PREY

The birds of prey are the bigger flesh-eating birds. They include the diurnal and nocturnal raptors and the scavenging vultures. Raptors are the butchers of the bird world and use talons to catch and kill their prey. All have strongly hooked bills and powerful feet with sharp talons, but the size, appearance and behaviour vary in the different species and this enables each species to fill a special niche and thus minimise competition. Vultures are the avian undertakers and seldom kill their own prey.

The giants

Eagles are the largest of the raptors – all are strongly built with exceptionally powerful talons.

Martial Eagles are aggressive and versatile hunters that hunt from great heights while soaring. Look for the dark breast and spotted white underparts to identify them. They prey on a variety of small to large mammals, birds and reptiles. These could be small antelope, hyraxes, hares, birds up to the size of a Kori Bustard, and reptiles such as monitor lizards.

The magnificent **Verreauxs' Eagles**[1] are confined to mountainous areas with cliffs where they nest on rock ledges. They are the most prey-specific of all large raptors as the greater part of their diet consists of rock hyraxes. However, they do take other mammals and game birds.

Crowned Eagles[2] have broad, short wings and long tails for manoeauvrability when pursuing prey in dense trees. It is an extremely powerful raptor with exceptionally large talons, enabling it to kill prey up to the size of a young bushbuck. It is also a successful hunter of monkeys. Large prey is dismembered and pieces are cached in trees.

Wahlberg's Eagles[1] are intra-African breeding migrants that usually arrive in August in southern Africa and commence breeding in September. Although often overlooked, they are the most common small eagles during summer. There is quite a colour variation between different individuals but they all have dark brown irises, black bills and yellow feet and ceres (fleshy coverings at the base of the upper beak). They prey on small mammals, birds, reptiles and insects and even prey as big as guineafowls and hares are caught.

African Hawk Eagles[2] are rapacious and dashing raptors that mainly prey on game birds but they take mammals and reptiles. They hunt from a perch or flying low over the ground. They frequently ambush prey at waterholes which is sometimes heavier than the birds themselves.

Tawny Eagles[3] vary in colour from dark brown to pale buff. They are typical savanna raptors that normally occur in pairs. They are opportunistic and take a variety of prey, ranging from medium-sized mammals to insects. They scavenge and are often the first to arrive at a carcass. A fair percentage of their prey is obtained through pirating, and fledglings are also taken from open nests.

The cry of the **African Fish Eagle** is often referred to as the 'call of Africa'. These iconic birds prefer water habitats, usually with big trees. They hunt from a perch and mainly take fish. They also pirate birds such as herons and storks, and sometimes catch waterbirds and their chicks.

Acrobat of the sky

The red face, legs and feet, distinctive plumage and the characteristic flight pattern can only be that of the master of soaring, the Bateleur.

A flying **Bateleur** rocking from side to side is a magnificent sight of the African bush. In this way they cover immense distances looking for food. They are scavengers to a large extent but do sometimes hunt birds and smaller prey.

Juvenile

Adult

The snake killers

Snake Eagles are specialist snake killers and they prey almost entirely on these reptiles, swallowing them whole. When nesting, they half ingest a snake and the nestlings pull it out when the parent arrives at the nest. They have long, heavily scaled legs and short toes, and large yellow eyes.

Black-chested Snake Eagles[1] have black heads and breasts and white underparts. They occur in lightly wooded and also in desert areas. They hunt while soaring, and drop down on their prey.

  Brown Snake Eagles[2] are uniformly brown eagles with light legs and large, yellow eyes. They frequently hunt from a perch, killing and swallowing prey on the ground.

The trapeze artist

In nature there is often a species that has developed special features to obtain food others cannot utilise. One such species is the African Harrier-hawk.

African Harrier-Hawks are unusual in both appearance and behaviour. They have yellow faces without plumage which turn red when they are excited, and their ankles seem to be double-jointed. They forage by hanging upside down by one foot while inserting the other flexible foot into hollows, cracks or birds' nests to get hold of prey. They are great robbers of weavers' nests.

The speedsters

This group includes raptors of the genus *Falconidae*. Falcons are striking birds and depend on speed to hunt down their avian prey. With their pointed wings and longish tails they are built for chasing birds in flight at great speed. They do, however, feed on small mammals, reptiles and insects.

The widespread and adaptable **Lanner Falcons**[1] hunt from a perch or in flight. In dry areas they favour waterholes where they ambush drinking birds that are then pursued at great speed. They sometimes hunt in pairs, one flushing the birds while the other does the catching. They also feed on mammals, reptiles and insects.

Peregrine Falcons[2] are regarded as the fastest animal on Earth. When they stoop, they fold their wings towards their tails and can reach speeds of almost 400km/h. They kill their prey by striking it with the hind claws or by biting through the neck. They carry their prey off in level flight by clinging to it with their claws.

The hovering kestrels

Although there are superficial similarities between falcons and kestrels, their habits differ considerably. Kestrels make less use of speed to catch prey. They often hunt from perches or by hovering.

The **Amur Kestrel**[1] is widespread and common. The **Rock Kestrel**[2] prefers open areas close to rocky outcrops. It has a varied diet which includes smaller mammals, reptiles, birds and invertebrates.

The bird snatchers

The bird snatchers are all from the genus *Accipiter* and include the sparrowhawks and goshawks. They all have short, rounded wings, long tails, long legs and thin, long toes with sharp claws. These characteristics make them ideally suited to catching birds in areas with trees. They inhabit savanna and forests, hunting from a concealed perch in trees and chasing prey in a bold and dashing way.

Little Sparrowhawks[1] are the smallest raptors in this group. They primarily catch small birds up to their own body weight. They are often found near water where they wait in ambush for birds coming to drink. They have a habit of sitting in water for long periods.

African Goshawks[2] are typical hawks of the forests and dense riverine bush. They hunt from dense cover and, although they mainly hunt birds, they also feed on mammals, reptiles, insects and even crabs.

Shrika[3] have uniform grey upper parts and bars on the belly and breast. They have red eyes, even as sub-adults. They are opportunistic raptors that often hunt at dusk, and have a more varied diet than other accipiters.

Its grey breast distinguishes the **Gabar Goshawk**[4] from other similar-looking raptors. It is widespread and enters built-up areas. It is able to catch birds heavier than itself and also robs birds' nests. When building a nest, it incorporates a nest of colonial spiders which then cover the nest with web.

The singing hawk

Although the **Dark Chanting Goshawk** has a similar build to other accipiters, it differs considerably with regard to behaviour and hunting methods. It is an opportunistic raptor which usually hunts from a perch. It feeds mainly on ground-living mammals, reptiles and insects but does catch birds (even those as large as Guineafowl).

Adult

Sub-adult

Soaring buzzards

This group includes medium-sized raptors with broad wings. They look like eagles but have bare legs. Some of them are long-distance migrants.

Common (Steppe) Buzzards are palearctic non-breeding migrants. It is one of southern Africa's most common medium-sized summer visiting raptors. They favour exposed perches, but form flocks at a good food source or when migrating. They largely feed on insects but catch small birds, mammals, frogs and other reptiles.

The specialist killers

Most raptors are opportunistic hunters that prey on a wide variety of prey items. There are, however, some that are very prey-specific and selective.

The small, handsome **Black-shouldered Kite**[1] is well known for its mouse-killing capabilities. Over 90% of its diet consists of rodents but it also catches small birds, reptiles and insects. It hunts either from a perch or by hovering. Breeding birds occur in pairs and non-breeding ones roost communally. They have the habit of wagging their tails up and down when excited.

Ospreys[2] have an almost worldwide distribution but are uncommon non-breeding visitors to southern Africa where they can be seen on large inland waterbodies and estuaries. They feed almost entirely on fish.

The flying kites

In summer the local raptor population of southern Africa is augmented by two similar-looking dark brown birds of prey that arrive in large numbers: the Yellow-billed Kite and the Black Kite. Both are migrants but only Yellow-billed Kites breed here. Both groups are gregarious, especially when there is a good food source such as termites.

The dark brown body, forked tail and yellow bill and legs are identifying features of the **Yellow-billed Kite**[2]. It feeds on smaller animals and can often be seen scavenging on road kills. When breeding they are found in pairs but form quite big flocks where there is a good food source.

LORDS OF THE NIGHT

This group includes all the nocturnal raptors but consists mainly of owls. When the sun sets, the diurnal raptors retire and their places are taken by owls and other nocturnal predators.

Owls and owlets

Owls have special adaptations to hunt at night. They all have superb night vision, their hearing is extremely acute (some species can catch prey relying on their hearing only) and their flight is silent so potential prey does not hear them approaching.

The huge **Verreaux's Eagle-owl** is the nocturnal equivalent of the diurnal big eagles. It preys on a variety of larger creatures such as hares, galagos, game birds and other birds, often taken from nests. Look for these owls in tall riparian trees.

Southern White-faced Owls[1] are widespread in a variety of savanna types. They feed on rodents but also take birds and arthropods such as insects and spiders.

Marsh Owls[2] favour moist grassland and marshy areas. They hunt by flying low and dropping suddenly on to their prey, which consists largely of small rodents.

The opportunistic **Spotted Eagle-owl**[3] occurs in a variety of habitats and has a cosmopolitan diet consisting of rodents, beetles, scorpions, birds, reptiles and even bats. It is often found in built-up areas such as rest camps in reserves and suburban gardens.

③

African Barred Owlets[1] prefer areas with tall trees and broad-leaved bushveld. They feed mainly on athropods but small vertebrates are caught.

African Scops-Owls[2] are masters of camouflage and during the day perch against stems or branches with half-closed eyes and are not easy to see. They feed primarily on insects but also catch small vertebrates.

The common and widespread **Western Barn Owl**[3] is strictly nocturnal. It hunts from a perch or by flying slowly over suitable habitat to locate prey. It feeds on rodents but other smaller vertebrates and insects are also taken. Prey is swallowed whole.

Pearl-spotted Owlets[4] are aggressive and bold hunters of birds (even bigger than themselves), rodents and insects. Their beautiful call can often be heard during the day.

Pel's Fishing Owls[1] are indeed a special sighting for any visitor to the wild. They are rare and occur in riverine bush along permanent rivers. As the name implies, they catch fish.

The well-camouflaged **African Wood-owl**[2] is a real forest bird more often heard than seen. It hunts by dropping on to prey consisting of insects and smaller vertebrates.

THE UNDERTAKERS

This group includes all the birds of prey that depend on scavenging to obtain their food. They do not have the specially adapted claws of other raptors to kill prey but some occasionally do so. It is important to note that all predatory birds are opportunistic and most will feed on carrion when available. Raptors such as the Bateleur and the Tawny Eagle often arrive first at a dead animal, and Yellow-billed Kites regularly patrol roads to pick up road kills.

The vultures

Vultures are large, carrion-feeding birds with strong, curved bills. Most of them have bare necks and heads. When the air has heated up sufficiently in the morning to cause thermals, they take to the wing to forage over a large area. The first one to notice potential food will fly down and the others will follow it in spiralling flight.

The large **White-backed Vultures** are the most common vulture in savanna areas. They breed and roost in trees and when not breeding are gregarious. They are aggressive at a carcass and feed mainly on the softer parts of large animals.

The pink, bare face and triangular shape of the head are identifying features of the rather handsome **White-headed Vulture**[1]. They start to fly earlier in the morning and often arrive first at a carcass. They also feed on the bodies of smaller mammals and birds and are known to kill their own prey. Like most raptors, they love termites.

The medium-sized **Hooded Vulture**[2] has a dark body, a pink face without plumage, and a slender bill. It cannot compete with other vultures at carcasses and picks up scraps and clean bones after others have finished. It also feeds on insects in dung and soil.

The very large, endangered **Cape Vulture**[3] is endemic to southern Africa. They are gregarious and nest and roost on precipitous cliff ledges from where they forage over the surrounding area. The eyes of adults are yellow and they have bluish necks.

The huge **Lappet-faced Vultures**[4] are dominant at a carcass. They have massive bills that enable them to rip open a carcass and to feed on tougher body parts such as skin, sinew and bone. Despite being mainly a scavenger, it is known to kill its own prey and will feed on emerging winged termites. They never arrive in big numbers at carcasses. The head is bare and has conspicuous skin folds.

BIRDS AT THE WATER

Little Egret

BIRDS AT THE WATER

A waterbird can be defined as a bird that feeds in or around
water. Their diet consists of aquatic life such as fish, frogs,
reptiles, crustaceans, molluscs, insects and aquatic vegetation.
The vast range of potential food items can be exploited only
if waterbirds have specific functional adaptations in form and
habits. It is therefore not surprising they have such a variety
of anatomical features such as the shape and size of their bills,
legs, necks and feet.

Flat-billed waterbirds

Where there are suitable stretches of water, expect to see one
or more species of duck or goose. All have webbed feet and
flattened bills. They feed on plant and animal matter.

Egyptian Geese are probably the most often seen of this family.
When not breeding or during moult, they form flocks. When breeding,
they form mating pairs and become aggressive and territorial.

Knob-billed (or Comb) Ducks[1] are associated with savanna and woodland regions where they forage on floodplains and at pans with surface vegetation. During breeding time, the males develop huge knobs on their bills.

Spur-winged Geese[2] are the largest in the family and can be distinguished by their metallic back plumage and white underparts. The male has a knob on its forehead. They are plant feeders and fly long distances to feed on suitable plants. During moult they congregate in great numbers on large stretches of open water .

White-faced Whistling Ducks[1] are widespread and can sometimes be seen in huge flocks. When breeding, they occur in pairs and small groups. Breeding pairs tend to preen each other often. They have a characteristic whistling call.

Look for **Fulvous Whistling Ducks**[2] in overgrown pans. They are gregarious and feed mainly by diving. They spend a lot of their time in large inactive groups.

African Pygmy-Geese[1] occur in subtropical areas where they prefer open water with water lilies. They feed almost exclusively on water lily seeds and flowers, but also on other plants and insects.

Cape Shovellers[2] are near-endemics favouring shallow water, obtaining food by dabbling below the water surface while swimming. The male has yellow eyes and the female brown eyes.

Yellow-billed Duck[3] are common over most of the region. They prefer open water and feed on plant material, including domestic grain. They obtain food in water by dabbling or up-ending.

The male **Southern Pochard**[4] has characteristic red eyes. It prefers open, clean water and gathers in large numbers at a good food source. It feeds on plant and animal matter.

Red-billed Teals[5] prefer dams and pans. They feed mainly on aquatic plants obtained by immersing the bill or by up-ending. They form huge flocks when not breeding.

1

Spear fishers

Herons and egrets are usually found near water and vary in size from small to very large. They have long legs, bills and necks which are kept folded when flying. They feed by wading and waiting patiently for prey. Their food consists of aquatic animals which they catch with their bills, either by spearing or grabbing, and then swallow whole.

Goliath Herons are the world's largest herons. They forage in the shallows of large bodies of water such as dams, pans and rivers, standing in the water for long periods waiting for prey that is speared with their huge bills.

Purple Herons[1] like dense vegetation, especially reeds. When they feel threatened, they turn their bills upwards to blend in with the vegetation. They use their sharp bills to spear their prey that is then swallowed whole.

Grey Herons[2] are common, widespread residents that prefer shallow water where they catch fish and frogs. They are normally solitary but sleep in groups in trees. The bill turns bright orange and the legs pinkish during breeding.

1

The all-white **Little Egrets**[1] have a black bill and legs, yellow feet, and plumes at the back of the head. They are active hunters in shallow water, often stirring the bottom with their feet.

Great Egrets[2] are all white with a long necks. Non-breeding adults have yellow bills, but during the breeding season these turn black and the ceres greenish colour. Their prey consists mainly of fish but they also take frogs, reptiles and insects.

The largely nocturnal **Black-crowned Night-Heron**[1] hunts from a low perch over water. It feeds on fish, frogs, crustaceans, molluscs, insects and spiders. Although often seen alone, they are normally gregarious when breeding or roosting.

Squacco Herons[2] prefer quiet waters with plenty of vegetation. They are shy and therefore easily overlooked. The white wings are conspicuous when they fly.

Black Herons[3] have the interesting habit of creating a canopy over their heads with their wings when fishing to eliminate reflections so that they can see better into the water. They favour marshes and wetlands.

Green-backed Herons[4] are small and short-necked. They prefer stretches of water with surrounding vegetation. When disturbed they will, like the Purple Heron, take an upright stance with bill pointed upwards and are then not readily seen. Interestingly, they use bait to attract prey.

4

The snappy grabber

Hamerkops are the only species in its family.

Hamerkops[1] snatch prey lightning-fast while wading or flying slowly over the water surface. They build huge nests with a small opening in trees or on rock ledges. Part of their display is to stand on each other's backs.

The probers

Storks are tall birds with large, long bills and long necks which are extended in flight. Of the eight species to be seen in the region, five are associated with water. The others are mainly grassland birds but may visit water when there is an available food source, or to drink and cool down. The Marabou Stork discussed under scavengers will, for instance, visit drying pools to feed on stranded fish.

Black Storks[1] are not often seen as they are uncommon and they are regarded as near-threatened. They have a preference for mountainous regions.

 Saddle-billed Storks[2] are huge birds with enormous black and red bills with yellow saddles. The males' eyes are dark and the females' yellow. They forage in shallows of larger bodies of water.

African Openbills[1] are all-black, glossy birds with a wide gap between the upper and lower parts of the bill, a special adaptation enabling them to feed on freshwater molluscs. The sharp lower mandibel is inserted into the shell to extract the contents. Mussels are sometimes left in the sun to open.

Yellow-billed Storks[2] are gregarious and forage in small groups. They move their bills from side to side feeling for prey disturbed by their feet, and they often open one wing to form a canopy when fishing.

Woolly-necked Storks[1] prefer wooded areas where they feed in whatever water they can find. They usually forage alone or in pairs in shallow water, and sometimes also in grassland.

The huge **Marabou Storks**[2] are often seen at a carcass where they will peck at vultures to get them out of the way. Like the vultures, they have a bare head and neck. They congregate at drying pools to feed on stranded fish, and eat insects and smaller vertebrates.

The odd-bills

This family has five species in southern Africa. They are large waders that feed on a variety of animal matter as well as carrion and detritus. The ibises often forage in grassland by probing. One ibis species, the Southern Bald Ibis, is a grassland bird. The ibises have long, downward-curving bills and those of the spoonbills are straight and spatulate.

The harsh, loud call of the **Hadeda Ibis**[1] is a well-known African sound. These birds are often seen at water, but spend most of their time foraging in grassland. They have adapted well to urban areas and favour lawns where they probe for food. They are opportunistic and will even scavenge from open dustbins.

  Glossy Ibises[2] have a wide distribution but are not found in the dry areas of the region. They feed on invertebrates and other animal matter in open waters and flooded grassland.

  African Sacred Ibises[3] prefer to forage in shallow water or grassland with wet soil and can often be seen on rubbish dumps. They have a very varied diet that could even include carrion as well as eggs, birds and young crocodiles.

  African Spoonbills[4] forage in shallow water by walking slowly and sweeping their bills from side to side or by probing mud. They feed on small fish, aquatic insects and crustacea, and breed in colonies.

The basket fishers

Pelicans are huge birds with long bills, hooked at the tip and with a highly distensible pouch underneath, all special adaptations to catch fish. They are widely distributed throughout the world and are found in marine and inland waters. Two species occur in southern Africa.

Great White Pelicans are common residents in their breeding area but will occasionally visit other bodies of water with food potential, soaring effortlessly to gain height. They fish in organised groups, driving fish into shallow water. They breed in colonies on the ground in places such as such as islands in protected areas.

The submarines

Four species of three different families obtain most of their prey by diving and swimming underwater. These include two cormorants, the African Darter and the Little Grebe. They have specific adaptations with regard to their bills and feet as well as feathers to enable them to pursue and catch prey underwater.

Reed Cormorants[1] are common wherever there are suitable stretches of water. In pursuing prey they dive underwater propelling themselves with their webbed feet. The sharp hook at the tip of their bills enables them to grab prey, which is swallowed whole after surfacing. Fish are always swallowed head first.

    Little Grebes[2] are seldom seen out of water. These nomadic birds fly at night to other suitable stretches of water. They can remain underwater for surprisingly long periods, catching small aquatic animals.

    White-breasted Cormorants[3] feed mainly on fish caught underwater. They catch surprisingly big fish, manoeuvring them in their bills before swallowing them head first. They prefer larger areas of water.

African Darters have similar hunting strategies to cormorants but they spear their prey with their long, sharp bills. They feed mainly on fish, but will catch frogs, insects and crustaceans. After fishing they sit on a perch and open their wings to dry.

Swimmers and divers

Many omnivorous aquatic birds forage by swimming and diving. They can often be seen resting at the water's edge, but most of their time is spent swimming.

Common Moorhens[1] are widespread residents and can be seen in most freshwater habitats with marginal vegetation. They have a varied diet of plants, insects, spiders, worms and tadpoles.

The uncommon and highly secretive **African Finfoot**[2] is indeed a highly sought-after species for birders and others visiting wilderness areas. It favours quiet stretches of water with overhanging vegetation.

Red-knobbed Coots[3] build floating platform nests on which they spend quite some time. They feed mainly on plant material.

The women's libbers

Two species of closely related families are extraordinary in the sense that the females behave differently to most birds. These are the African Jacana and the Greater Painted Snipe. In both cases the females are larger than the males. The Greater Painted Snipe takes it a step further – the female is more richly coloured. The females of both species mate with different males and leave most of the breeding and parental care to the males.

The shy **Greater Painted Snipe**[1] prefers wetlands with lots of vegetation where it forages for invertebrates and seeds. The richly coloured female is polyandrous and leaves most of the parental care to the male.

   African Jacanas[2] have extraordinarily long toes that enable them to walk on floating vegetation. They feed on invertebrates and seeds. The male holds the eggs under its wings when sitting on the nest and also carries the fledging under its wings.

Plovers

Plovers are small waders with shortish legs and bills. They favour shallow water or open areas next to water. They breed on the ground and use very little nest material. The chicks are precocial (i.e. they move and feed directly after hatching).

Common Ringed Plovers[1] are long-distance migrants (up to 12 000 km). They breed over a wide area in the northern hemisphere and some visit southern Africa as non-breeding migrants.

Kittlitz's Plovers[2] are less water-bound than other plovers and can sometimes be seen foraging in open areas away from water. They lay their eggs in a mere scrape, and when they feel threatened will quickly cover the eggs and move away.

Three-banded Plovers[3] are quite common and can be seen at pans, rivers, dams and temporary rainwater pools. They forage at the water's edge or in shallow water and feed on crustaceans, insects, worms and molluscs.

Lapwings

Lapwings have longer legs than plovers and are larger. Not all the lapwing species are associated with water. You can expect to see four species at water or in damp places close to water.

African Wattled Lapwings[1] are seen close to water in moist, grassy areas, on mud and sand banks or on the shoreline. They feed on frogs, fish and insects. They have conspicuous spurs on their wings.

White-crowned Lapwings[2] are localised birds, preferring bigger rivers where they forage on mud and sand banks or on the shoreline. They feed on frogs, fish and insects. They have conspicuous spurs on their wings.

Blacksmith Lapwings[3] are widespread and can often be seen foraging in shallow water or on the shoreline. Their call is a characteristic metallic 'klink, klink, klink' like a hammer on an anvil, hence the name.

The secretive squad

There are quite a number of birds that forage in shallow water with plants. All these bird are secretive and not easily seen. They can best be observed by sitting in a hide or vehicle next to water.

African Purple Swamphens[1] (Purple Gallinules) are colourful, shy birds that forage in reeds, rushes and sedges. They feed on plants as well as a variety of animal matter such as insects, nestlings, eggs and even carrion.

African Crakes[2] are uncommon breeding migrants with fluctuating numbers, depending on rainfall. They prefer water with lots of vegetation and even temporarily flooded grassland.

The **African Snipe**'s[3] bill is more than twice the length of its head. It prefers shallow water in brackish or freshwater wetlands where it feeds on aquatic insects and other smaller creatures.

Black Crakes[4] are not as shy as others of their family and can regularly be seen where there is suitable water for foraging. They feed on a variety of arthropods but also small fish, bird nestlings, eggs and some seeds and water plants.

International visitors

A multitude of non-breeding palearctic waders visits southern Africa annually. They are all brown, inconspicuous birds in their non-breeding region, but many of them develop elaborate breeding plumage where they breed.

Common Sandpipers[1] are smallish waders occurring on almost any shoreline. They feed on crustaceans, insects, molluscs and even fish fry. They breed in Eurasia and Japan and migrate south to southern Africa and even Australia.

Common Greenshanks[2] can be distinguished by their slightly up-turned bills and greenish legs. They occur widely in inland and marine water habitats.

The backs of **Ruffs**[3] are heavily mottled and their bills shortish and thick at the base. The male is considerably larger than the female and in their breeding grounds it develops a striking plumage.

The olive-brown spotted back and yellowish legs are characteristic of **Wood Sandpipers**[4]. They forage in shallow water or moist grass. They breed in northern Europe and Asia but some remain in the south throughout the year.

Avocets and stilts

The birds in this group have particularly long legs, thin bills and black and white plumage. They inhabit shallow water where they feed on a variety of aquatic animals. At times they are found in large numbers in suitable habitats. Only two species occur in southern Africa.

Pied Avocets[1] have long, grey legs, upcurved, thin bills and black and white plumage. They forage by wading in shallow water and sweeping their bills from side to side over the surface. They feed on invertebrates, small fish, seeds and plants.

The long, red legs and dark backs of **Black-winged Stilts**[2] are characteristic. These highly nomadic birds forage by wading quickly and catching edible items on the surface, or with their heads under the water. They feed on a variety of invertebrates and seeds.

Thick-knees

Thick-knees are lapwing-like birds with big eyes, thick knees and they have no hind toes. They are nocturnal birds. There are two species in the region, with only one associated with water: the Water Thick-knee.

Water Thick-knees occur in the wetter parts of the region at rivers, dams, pans, mangrove swamps and beaches. They feed on insects, crabs, frogs, molluscs and small fish.

Wagtails

Wagtails get their name by their habit of wagging their rather long tails up and down.

Cape Wagtails[1] can be seen at dams and rivers, and have adapted well to urban areas.

African Pied Wagtails[2] are the largest of the wagtails. These black and white birds can be seen along rivers and in other wet places, and sometimes also in gardens. They feed mainly on smaller arthropods.

Filter feeders

Flamingos have very long legs and necks and actually feed with their heads upside down while filtering out small organisms with thin bony plates in their downward-curving bills. They are gregarious and highly nomadic, flying long distances to good food sources in marine and inland waters.

Lesser Flamingos[1] are pinkish birds with dark bills. They occur in big flocks (often with Greater Flamingos) in open saline or brackish water. Their diet is more vegetarian, mainly microscopic algae and diatoms.

  Greater Flamingos[2] are white with red on the wings and dark primary feathers. They often forage in large flocks for small aquatic invertebrates and algae in brackish water. They have a wide distribution.

The dive-bombers

Some fish-eating birds catch their prey by diving into the water. They use a perch from which to scan the water, but some do so by hovering. Fish are caught with talons like the African Fish Eagle, the Osprey and the Pel's Fishing-Owl, while others such as the kingfishers catch fish with their bills.

Malachite Kingfishers are quite common over the eastern part of the region. These strikingly colourful little jewels of the waterways prefer water with marginal vegetation. They perch low over water in trees, bushes or reeds and dive for prey. They feed on tadpoles, fish, insects and crustaceans.

Pied Kingfisher[1] are common at rivers, lakes and dams. They fish either from a perch or by hovering with the body held in an almost upright position. They feed mainly on fish.

The **Giant Kingfisher**[2] is the largest kingfisher in southern Africa. They prefer perennial rivers and hunt from a perch such as a rock or low branch, seldom by hovering. They prey on fish, crabs and insects.

Western Cattle Egret

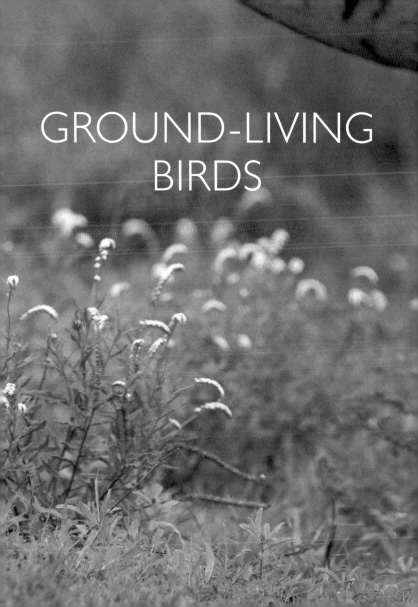

GROUND-LIVING BIRDS

GROUND-LIVING BIRDS

This section includes all the terrestrial birds. A terrestrial bird can be described as a bird that obtains its food at ground level and breeds on the ground. Most ground-living birds are not easily seen, as they have subdued colours for camouflage. Because of their foraging habits they also fly less often than other birds.

The Giant

The largest of all birds, the **Common Ostrich**, is a terrestrial and flightless bird that obtains all its food, consisting of plant material, at ground level. They occur in flocks when not breeding.

The terrestrial hornbill

Although **Southern Ground Hornbills** roost and mostly nest in trees, they forage while walking on the ground. They feed on insects, molluscs, frogs, reptiles (including snakes and tortoises) and mammals as large as hares.

The Hunter-bird

Secretarybirds prefer open areas that they patrol, looking for prey such as insects, birds, reptiles, mammals and amphibians. They subdue larger prey with hard downward blows of their feet.

Bustards and korhaans

This family is strictly terrestrial. They have long necks and legs, with short toes (the hind toe is absent) and are cryptically coloured. During breeding time the males get involved in elaborate displays.

Black-bellied Bustards[1] occur in a variety of habitats. In summer the males often call from an elevated perch. They feed on insects and plants.

The **Red-crested Korhaan**[2] male performs a spectacular display flight – flying straight up into the air and then tumbling down as if shot. The red crest is also opened in display but is otherwise seldom seen.

Kori Bustards are the heaviest birds capable of flying. They prefer open savanna where they feed on insects, reptiles and fruit. The Afrikaans name gompou ('gum peacock') is from its habit of eating tree gum or resin.

Herons and storks

Although most heron and stork species are aquatic birds, two species of each group are terrestrial and prefer open areas not necessarily close to water. These are Black-headed Herons, Cattle Egrets, Abdim's Storks and White Storks.

Cattle Egrets[1] are common over the whole area and their range has expanded worldwide. They often accompany grazing animals to catch insects and other prey disturbed by the grazers.

Abdim's Storks[2] are non-breeding intra-African migrants that visit the region in large numbers. They are insectivorous, and large flocks can be seen at insect outbreaks such as the emergence of termites after rain.

White Storks[3] are common and widespread non-breeding summer visitors from the northern hemisphere. They favour grassland, cultivated fields and open woodland.

Black-headed Herons[4] are common residents and widespread in grassland areas. They feed primarily on insects but also catch vertebrates.

Long-legged runners

Birds in this group are all very terrestrial, obtaining all their food at ground level, and they also breed on the ground.

Spotted Thick-knees[1] are common, widespread residents. They favour open areas, including parks and sports fields in built-up areas.

Temminck's Coursers[2] are migratory. They prefer open over-grazed and burnt grassland where they forage for insects and seeds.

Crowned Lapwings[3] are common and favour open areas and short grassland, as well as in urban areas. They feed on insects, especially termites.

The resident population of **Bronze-winged Coursers**[4] is augmented in summer by a migratory population. They are largely nocturnal and feed on insects.

Grassland larks

A huge area of southern Africa consists of grassland and semi-desert, and it is therefore not surprising many lark species make this their home. They are all cryptically coloured to blend in with their exposed habitat. They eat insects and seeds.

Sabota Larks[1] are widespread and common. They prefer open savanna where seeds form about 60% of their diet, and invertebrates the rest.

Dusky Larks[2] are non-breeding intra-African migrants visiting the northern part of the region. They are mainly insectivorous.

The clear, loud call of the **Rufous-naped Lark**[3] is a typical summer sound in open areas. These common residents feed on insects and seeds.

Other grassland favourites

Pipits and longclaws are also birds of grassy habitats.
Pipits are extremely hard to identify as they look similar to
longclaws, except for the splash of colour which the latter
has on its breast.

African Pipits[1] are common residents, especially in the highveld
grasslands. They feed primarily on insects.

Yellow-throated Longclaws[2] favour areas with shortish grass, in
which they forage for insects. They have a clear, loud call, usually
from a perch in a tree.

Wild chickens

Francolins, spurfowls and guineafowls are domestic poultry-like birds that do all their foraging on the ground. They are reluctant to fly and sustain flight only for a short distance.

Natal Spurfowls[1] are common bushveld birds occurring in a variety of habitats. They are plant eating but supplement their diet in summer with insects.

   Swainson's Spurfowls[2] are common and widespread. They call regularly from a perch at dawn and dusk. They eat a variety of plant matter with more insects in summer.

2

Crested Francolins[1] are true bushveld birds, favouring dense, bushy vegetation. Their duet call early in the morning and late afternoon is a typical bushveld sound.

Coqui Francolins[2] like habitats with tall grass in the northern, wetter savanna region. They are the smallest of the southern African francolins.

Shelley's Francolins[3] are fairly common and occur in open savanna. In winter they feed mostly on plants but in summer they increasingly take insects.

❸

Crested Guineafowls[1] favour thicket and forest edges in well-wooded areas. They forage by sctratching in leaf litter and roost in groups in trees.

Helmeted Guineafowls[2] are highly gregarious and are common over most of southern Africa. During the breeding season they usually form pairs.

Nightjars

Nightjars become active at dusk when they start hawking insects in flight, and are often seen on roads during night drives. Their plumage is extremely cryptic. During the day they roost on the ground, rocks or branches, relying on their camouflage to avoid being seen. They lay their eggs on the ground.

Square-tailed Nightjars[1] are common residents in the lowveld. They become active at dawn and hawk prey from the ground or a perch, but also in flight.

Fiery-necked Nightjars[2] hawk insects from a perch. Their characteristic and distinctive call can be heard at dusk and dawn, and on moonlit nights.

European Nightjars[3] are common and widespread non-breeding migrants to the region. They hawk insects at twilight and moonlight.

2

3

BIRDS IN TREES

Bennet's Woodpecker

BIRDS IN TREES

A vast area of southern Africa is clothed in bushes and trees, an area with the largest percentage of bird species. This diversity is possible because of the variety of different habitats offered. Many species use trees for nesting or as perches to catch prey, but a considerable number obtain most of their food in trees such as seeds, fruit, nectar, leaves or tree-living invertebrates and vertebrates.

Barbets and Woodpeckers

Although barbets and woodpeckers chisel out their nests in dry tree trunks or branches and both have two forward-facing and two backward-facing toes, they do not belong to the same family and their biology is very different.

Barbets have large, thick, serrated bills. They are mainly fruit eating but also take insects and other smaller prey.

Woodpeckers fill a special niche in nature. They have strong, chisel-like bills to drill into dry wood to get to insects and borers and then use their long and mobile tongues to extract the prey. Some species feed on the ground.

The beautiful duet of a pair of **Black Collared Barbets** is a typical bushveld sound. They are to a large extent fruit-eating but do prey on insects.

Acacia Pied Barbets[1] are widespread and common in dry savanna areas. They feed on fruit, seeds and nectar, and will even feed on fat off bones.

Crested Barbets[2] often feed on the ground, looking for termites and other insects. Their call is a penetrating trill lasting up to 30 seconds.

Golden-tailed Woodpeckers[1] are common residents in thornveld, woodland and even forests. They feed on insects, mainly ants and their larvae.

Bennett's Woodpeckers[2] often feed on the ground eating primarily ants, their eggs and pupae.

The widespread **Cardinal Woodpecker**[3] (see next spread) is a small bird with a brown forecrown in both sexes.

Hornbills

All hornbills have huge, downward curving bills. They have a mixed diet including fruit, insects and vertebrates. During the breeding season the females of all species except the Southern Ground Hornbill and Monteiro's Hornbill are enclosed with mud and faeces in a natural tree cavity with a narrow slit left for feeding. Some time after the hatching of the fledglings, the entrance is opened and the female comes out, the cavity is closed again and both male and female feed the chicks until they can emerge.

Southern Red-billed Hornbills[1] prefer dry, open woodland in the northern part of the region. They mostly eat insects.
   Southern Yellow-billed Hornbills[2] are common and widespread and can often be seen in rest camps and picnic sites.

❷

Look for **Trumpeter Horn-bills**[1] in treetops where they feed on fruit, particularly figs.

Crowned Hornbills[2] feed mainly on fruit and prefer dense vegetation.

African Grey Hornbills[3] tend to forage in trees and are not often seen on the ground.

Hoopoes and scimitarbills

Hoopoes and scimitarbills have long, slender, downward-curving bills suitable for probing for food. They feed mainly on insects and smaller vertebrae. The Wood-hoopoes and Common Scimitarbills also feed on nectar. They nest in natural cavities and holes, often in unused woodpecker and barbet nests.

African Hoopoes[1] are handsome birds that forage on the ground where they walk around actively probing the soil for prey.

   Green Wood-hoopoes[2] are gregarious, noisy and active. They move about on trunks and branches where they probe holes, cracks and cavities for prey.

   Common Scimitarbills[3] normally forage on their own, probing cavities for prey with their long, thin bills. They visit flowers for nectar.

The insect spies

Quite a number of bird species use trees as perches from where they scan their surroundings for prey. These include many of the raptors, rollers, bee-eaters, drongos, the non-aquatic kingfishers, some shrikes and flycatchers.

Lilac-breasted Rollers can be regarded as iconic birds of the bush-veld. Their bright, spectacular plumage can best be admired when they are in flight.

Purple Rollers[1] are not as common in the region. Their prey includes a large number of insects but bigger vertebrates such as birds and mice are also caught.

European Rollers[2] are non-breeding migrants arriving in early summer in great numbers to benefit from the temporary explosion of insect numbers during the rainy season.

There are two distinct populations of **European Bee-eaters**[1] in southern Africa: one a non-breeding population and the other a breeding population in the dry western regions. They hunt while flying and their calls can often be heard before you can see them.

   Southern Carmine Bee-eaters[2] are highly gregarious and flocks of hundreds of birds are common, especially in their breeding area. They breed to the north of South Africa and migrate southwards after breeding. They prey on large flying insects and they even feed on highly toxic blister beetles.

During the day **Little Bee-eaters**[1] hunt alone or in pairs but roost in groups in a tightly packed row on a branch at night.

White-fronted Bee-eaters[2] are common widespread residents. Look for them along rivers in the bushveld and for their breeding holes in riverbanks. They hunt from a perch and catch flying insects in the air or on the surface of water.

1

❷

The aggressive and bold **Fork-tailed Drongo** is common and wide-spread. It feeds on a variety of food items including insects, smaller vertebrates, ticks as well as nectar. It often accompanies grazing animals to catch the insects they disturb in the grass, and it also robs other insect-eaters of their prey.

The **African Pygmy Kingfisher**[1] is a breeding intra-African visitor which migrates at night. It prefers habitats with denser vegetation.

Woodland Kingfishers[2] are common breeding visitors. They are highly vocal and their call is a characteristic sound of the bushveld during summer. They perch low down in trees, scanning the ground for prey.

The **Striped Kingfisher**[1] is common and widespread, especially where there are large trees. It is a small kingfisher, unobtrusive when not calling and feeds on insects and small reptiles.

   Brown-hooded Kingfishers[2] are common residents in all woodland types, as well as gardens and parks. They feed on insects and smaller vertebrates, including small birds.

Lesser Grey Shrikes[1] are summer visitors from Europe and Asia that do not breed in Africa. They prefer dry, open areas. Like the Common Fiscal, they impale prey on thorns.

Southern White-crowned Shrikes[2] prefer open woodland. They perch conspicuously in groups or solitary in trees from where they look out for insects.

The **Common Fiscal**[3] is widespread and common in open areas with scattered trees and shrubs, including urban gardens and parks. Like the Lesser Grey, it also impales its prey on thorns and for that reason, one of its common names is Jackie Hangman.

3

Magpie Shrikes[1] hunt in small groups by perching low and catching prey on the ground.

   Red-backed Shrikes[2] are common non-breeding summer visitors to open savanna. They are specialist insect catchers.

❷

Fiscal Flycatchers[1] look very similar to the Common Fiscal.

Ashy Flycatchers[2] are confined to the eastern region of southern Africa. They use a low perch to hawk insects in flight.

African Paradise Flycatchers[3] are breeding migrants to denser bush-veld areas. Some remain all year round in the lower, eastern regions. The male has an exquisite orange-rust tail twice the body length.

Spotted Flycatchers[4] are common non-breed-ing migrants from the northern hemisphere. They feed mainly on in-sects caught in flight and occasionally small fruit.

The fruit eaters

Many bird species forage in trees for tree-living organisms, plant material and fruit. Carnivorous species go from tree to tree looking for suitable prey, and the fruit-eaters concentrate on trees with ripening fruit. There are, however, many species that feed on both animal and plant matter.

Most pigeons are seed-eaters but some species are primarily fruit eating. Of these, the African Green Pigeon is the most likely to be seen on game drives. **African Green Pigeons**[1] prefer dense vegetation with fruiting trees, especially wild figs. They gather in small numbers at a suitable food source.

Grey Go-away-birds[2] (see next spread) are common in dry savanna areas where their highly vocal call is a well-known sound. They feed on fruit, buds, flowers, nectar and invertebrates.

Meyer's Parrots[1] favour dry savanna woodland where they feed on fruit and fruit kernels, nuts, seeds and flowers.

Brown-headed Parrots[2] occur in the eastern low-lying savanna. They feed on fruit, seeds, flowers, leaves and nectar.

Purple-crested Turacos[3] are beautiful birds that prefer dense woodland and riparian bush where they feed on fruit and leaf buds. The bright red primary feathers can best be seen when they are in flight.

Red-faced Mousebirds[1] are widespread in Africa and occur in gardens. Their diet consists mainly of fruit but they also eat leaves, flowers and nectar.

Speckled Mousebirds[2] occur in the eastern bushveld regions. They feed on fruit, leaves and nectar but will take insects such as winged termites.

The everything eaters

Omnivorous birds make up the bulk of arboreal birds. As a result of their diverse diet, they are more adaptable and therefore occur in larger numbers – some of the most common birds are in this group.

The common endemic **Cape White-eye**[1] occurs in most wooded habitats. They forage restlessly in small groups in trees for small insects and fruit but also join sunbirds to feed on nectar.

Sombre Greenbuls[2] prefer dense thicket where they are more often heard than seen. They forage at all levels of the vegetation for fruit, insects, leaf buds and snails. They visit aloe flowers for nectar.

Dark-capped Bulbuls[3] are abundant in the eastern wetter savanna and are common garden birds. They have a cosmopolitan diet consisting of fruit, flowers, insects, small vertebrates and nectar.

Black-headed Orioles[4] (see next spread) normally forage for insects and fruit in the top of trees from where they call their melodious notes. When aloes are in flower they come down to feed on nectar and are more easily seen.

3

4

Spectacled Weavers[1] forage by creeping in trees and shrubs. They form pairs and do not change plumage during the breeding season. Their food consists of invertebrates, fruit, seeds and nectar.

  Red-headed Weavers[2] forage off plant surfaces for insects, spiders, seeds and fruit. They build untidy nests of twigs, sticks and leaves.

Red-winged Starlings[1] prefer rocky areas. They forage in trees or on the ground. Their food consists of fruit, insects, ectoparasites, lizards and aloe nectar.

Greater Blue-eared Starlings[2] are fruit- and insect eaters. They sometimes form large flocks.

Meve's Starlings[3] are common in northern woodland regions with mopane and baobab, and can regularly be seen along the larger rivers. They roost in large flocks.

When not breeding **Cape Glossy Starlings**[4] move in small flocks. They feed in trees and on the ground. They eat fruit, insects and nectar.

Burchell's Starlings[5] occur in open acacia savanna. They forage on bare ground for insects and smaller vertebrates or look for fruit in trees.

Wattled Starlings[1] are gregarious birds and nomadic, moving from one suitable food source to another. They feed on fruit, nectar and invertebrates.

   Violet-backed Starlings[2] are breeding intra-African migrants. They forage mainly in trees for fruit and insects, but also hawk flying insects.

Pied Crows[1] can sometimes be seen at carcasses and road kills, and they often visit dumpsites. They are, however, also plant-eaters and catch a variety of animals.

Carnivorous foragers

The great majority of tree-living (arboreal) birds feed on smaller prey items such as insects, spiders, worms and smaller vertebrates. They feed either by moving around in trees and shrubs, or by foraging on the ground.

Brubrus[1] usually forage for insects high in trees. They are more often heard than seen.

The highly vocal **Rattling Cisticola's**[2] call must be one of the most characteristic sounds of the bushveld. They are insectivorous.

Long-billed Crombecs[3] have short tails. They forage for insects on trunks, leaves and branches, working their way up from the bottom to the top.

Chin-spot Batisses[4] are common residents and can often be seen foraging in pairs in trees. The name is derived from the chestnut chin spot of the female.

White-crested Helmet-shrikes[1] are gregarious. They forage in groups for insects, spiders and small vertebrates at all levels and on the ground.

Although **Orange-breasted Bush-shrikes**[2] are very vocal, they are not easy to see. They forage for their insect prey in the woodland canopy.

Grey-headed Bush-shrikes[3] have a varied diet ranging from insects to reptiles, birds and mammals. They wedge larger prey in a tree fork and then dismember it with their heavy bills.

Black-backed Puffbacks[1] forage higher up in trees where they glean insects from trunks, branches and leaves. Males have a spectacular display, raising their white back feathers to create a puff.

Black-crowned Tchagras[2] are common in savanna areas. They feed on insects and smaller reptiles.

Southern Boubous[3] are vocal and pairs keep in contact by duetting. They feed on insects, birds' eggs, fledglings, reptiles, smaller mammals and even fruit.

❸

The **Diderick Cuckoo**[1] is the most common of the three green cuckoos. They are intra-African migrants and leave eggs in the nests of bishops, weavers and sparrows.

The **Jacobin Cuckoo's**[2] loud call can be heard from October to May. They parasitise bulbuls and Common Fiscals.

Great Spotted Cuckoos[3] are summer visitors to the region. They are conspicuous and noisy. Prey consists mainly of hairy caterpillars. They use crows and starlings as hosts.

Red-capped Robin-Chats[1] prefer dense vegetation along rivers and round dams. They are excellent songsters and impressive mimics artist.

The **White-browed Robin-Chat**[2] can be regarded as one of the best avian songsters in the world. It forages mainly on the ground during the early morning and late afternoon.

White-throated Robin-Chats[3] favour thicket in the eastern savanna region. They feed on insects and occasionally fruit.

Mocking Cliff Chats[4] occur in rocky terrain in the savanna. They feed on insects, fruit and aloe nectar.

Arrow-marked Babblers live in close-knit family groups. They forage on the ground for a variety of invertebrates and vertebrates.

Kurrichane Thrushes[1] are found in the eastern bushveld areas and are also common garden birds. They feed on insects, worms, spiders and small reptiles. They expose prey by tossing leaves aside.

Groundscraper Thrushes[2] forage in open areas, including lawns in parks and gardens. Their food consists largely of insects and earthworms.

Burchell's Coucals favour riparian vegetation with long grass. They like to sun themselves on an exposed perch in the morning, and feed on a wide range of vertebrates and invertebrates.

Oxpeckers

Oxpeckers spend most of their time on larger mammals feeding on ectoparasites such as ticks and insects, loose skin and even blood of the host animal. They do, however, roost in trees and often nest in holes in trees.

Yellow-billed Oxpeckers[1] prefer to forage on large mammals, and can often be seen on buffaloes.

Red-billed Oxpeckers[2] are more common and widespread in bushveld areas. They occur in small groups and use giraffe, antelope, buffalo, zebra and even domestic cattle as hosts.

1

Swallows

Swallows are diurnal hunters of flying insects. They have small, flattened bills which can open very wide. Their slender, streamlined bodies and long, pointed wings allow them to stay in the air for long periods, hawking insects. Many are migratory. Although their food is obtained while flying, they often rest and roost in trees.

Red-breasted Swallows[1] are locally common breeding intra-African migrants from tropical Africa.

Barn (European) Swallows[2] are by far the most common swallow in summer. At night they roost in large numbers in reed beds. They are migrants that breed in the northern hemisphere.

Lesser Striped Swallows[3] are common breeding migrants in the eastern low-lying region. They are mainly insectivorous but also eat fruit and small seeds.

The seed crackers

Seedeaters are found throughout southern Africa in all habitats. Grasslands come to mind when considering seedeaters but even some plants on the forest floor provide seeds for them. Although they spend a lot of time feeding on the ground, they roost and nest in trees and shrubs. Many of the smaller birds have short conical bills adapted for cracking open seeds. Most of the species nest in trees, shrubs, tall grass and reeds, but the greater part of their food is obtained on the ground. As seedeaters they have to drink regularly, and waiting at drinking places is recommended if you want to observe these birds, especially the small, unobtrusive species.

In summer the male **White-winged Widowbird**[1] displays from an exposed perch or by flying slowly. They occur in vlei areas with rank vegetation.

    Southern Red Bishops[2] are common residents over a large area. They nest in colonies, in reed beds in or on the edge of water.

❷

Southern Masked-weavers[1] are widespread and common in open savanna and also in gardens. They are gregarious when feeding and breed in colonies, but sometimes a solitary male builds a number of nests.

Village Weavers[2] are common in the eastern savanna regions. They are gregarious and breed in colonies in trees and reeds.

Red-billed Buffalo-weavers[3] build huge, untidy nests with thorny twigs. They form small flocks and forage on the ground for seeds, fruit and insects.

Lesser Masked-weavers[4] are gregarious in small flocks at all times and breed in colonies in trees, often over water. They feed on insects, seeds and nectar.

Red-billed Queleas[5] are abundant and flocks can number hundreds of thousands. After good rain in an area, they build an enormous number of nests there.

Red-billed Firefinches[1] favour acacia savanna where they can be seen feeding on the ground in clearings and on road verges. They eat seed but also take some insects.

Blue Waxbills[2] are common in eastern bushveld regions. They forage in small flocks on the ground for seeds and insects, and regularly visit waterholes.

Violet-eared Waxbills[3] occur in dry savanna. They are often seen at waterholes where they gather with other seedeaters to drink.

Green-winged Pytillias[4] forage in pairs or small flocks in clearings for seeds and insects. They are not easily seen but look for them at a drinking place as they drink regularly.

Common Waxbills[5] are gregarious and prefer rank vegetation. They forage on the ground for seeds and insects, or in trees for fruit.

Jameson's Firefinch[6] is a common resident in the eastern savanna regions where it favours rank vegetation, feeding on seeds and small insects.

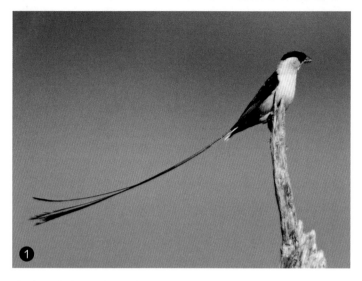

Shaft-tailed Whydahs[1] favour dry acacia savanna. They generally use Violet-eared Waxbills as hosts.

Breeding **Pin-tailed Whydah**[2] males are extremely aggressive towards all other birds at a feeding place. They use waxbills as hosts to rear their young.

Southern Grey-headed Sparrows[1] are widespread in dry savanna areas and often enter human settlements.

Red-headed Finches[2] are highly nomadic and gregarious when not breeding.

Yellow-fronted Canaries[1] are common in throughout Kruger.

Brimstone Canaries[2] occur in the eastern montane and coastal areas. They do eat seeds but include more fruit in their diet.

Golden-breasted Buntings[3] occur in bushveld, riverine bush and also in gardens. They feed on insects, seeds and buds.

Cinnamon-breasted Buntings[4] favour rocky and broken terrain. They feed on the ground, eating seeds as well as some insects.

1

The soft-billed seedeaters

In southern Africa some species of doves and pigeons are quite common. Most feed on the ground looking for seeds. Not having the seed-cracking bills of other seedeaters, they ingest small stones to assist digestion.

Namaqua Doves[1] are birds of the dry bushveld. They feed on small seeds.

Laughing Doves[2] are abundant and widespread. They feed on seeds and occasionally fruit and insects.

Cape Turtle Doves[3] have a wide distribution and are common, especially in the drier areas.

Emerald-spotted Wood-doves[4] are real bushveld birds occurring in the eastern region. They feed on seeds but also fruit and insects.

African Mourning Doves[5] are seed-eating and have a smaller distribution than the other two turtle doves.

Red-eyed Doves[6] prefer well-developed woodland. They feed on seeds and small fruit.

Speckled Pigeons[7] breed on rock ledges.

Sunbirds

When considering nectar as a food item, sunbirds and sugarbirds come to mind. There are, however, many other insect- and seed-eating birds that will relish a good source of nectar, especially from aloes. Sunbirds are small nectar-feeding birds with long, down-curved bills and long extendable tongues. The males are brightly coloured with a metallic green or bronze sheen, and the females are dull and difficult to identify. They are active and feed mainly on nectar, but fruit and some arthropods are also eaten.

Amethyst Sunbirds[1] are restless and aggressive, and often hover to extract nectar.

  Collared Sunbirds[2] are small, and both the male and female are brightly coloured. The male can be distinguished by its green and blue throat. They include small fruit in their diet.

The sooty black **Scarlet-chested Sunbird**[1] male often sings from a conspicuous perch high in a tree. These sunbirds feed on spiders, insects and nectar, especially of aloe and coral tree flowers.

White-bellied Sunbirds[2] are also small and occur in acacia savanna and drier woodland. They feed on nectar of many plants and are common visitors to flowering aloes.

Marico Sunbirds[3] are common and widespread in acacia savanna, riverine bush and gardens. The males are restless and aggressive.

Purple-banded Sunbirds[4] look very much like Marico Sunbirds but are smaller with a narrower breast band and shorter bill.

1

Blacksmith Lapwing

THUMBNAILS
of Kruger birds

134
Crested Guineafowl
Kuifkoptarentaal

112
Common Ostrich
Volstruis

135
Helmeted Guineafowl
Gewone Tarentaal

105
Greater Flamingo
Grootflamink

104
Lesser Flamingo
Kleinflamink

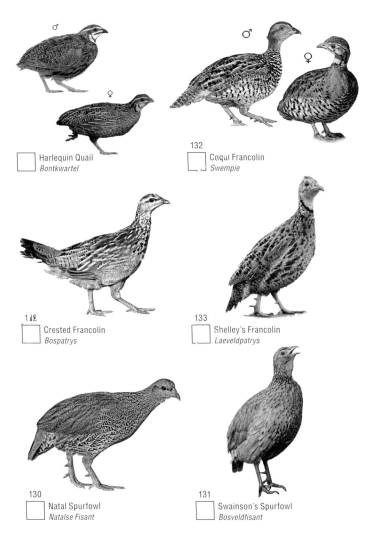

♂

♀

Harlequin Quail
Bontkwartel

132 Coqui Francolin
Swempie

♂

♀

131 Crested Francolin
Bospatrys

133 Shelley's Francolin
Laeveldpatrys

130 Natal Spurfowl
Natalse Fisant

131 Swainson's Spurfowl
Bosveldfisant

235

♂

♀

☐ Southern Pochard
Bruineend

☐ African Black Duck
Swarteend

59
☐ Fulvous Whistling Duck
Fluiteend

56
☐ Knob-billed Duck
Knobbeleend

☐ White-backed Duck
Witrugeend

58 White-faced
☐ Whistling Duck
Nonnetjie-eend

♂

♀

Yellow-billed Duck
Geelbekwitreier

African Pygmy Goose
Dwerggans

54
Egyptian Goose
Kolgans

57
Spur-winged Goose
Wildemakou

Hottentot Teal
Gevlekte Eend

Red-billed Teal
Rooibekeend

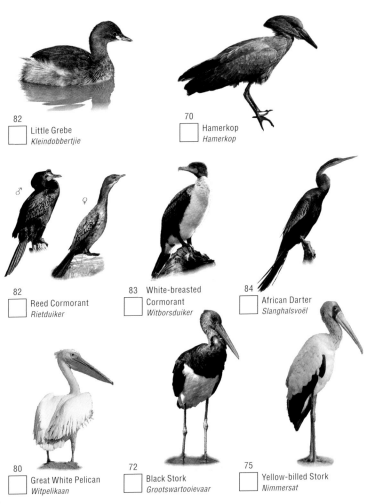

82 ☐ Little Grebe
Kleindobbertjie

70 ☐ Hamerkop
Hamerkop

82 ☐ Reed Cormorant
Rietduiker

83 ☐ White-breasted
Cormorant
Witborsduiker

84 ☐ African Darter
Slanghalsvoël

80 ☐ Great White Pelican
Witpelikaan

72 ☐ Black Stork
Grootswartooievaar

75 ☐ Yellow-billed Stork
Nimmersat

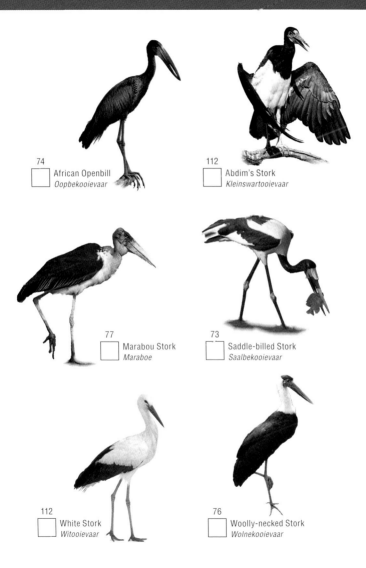

74 African Openbill
Oopbekooievaar

112 Abdim's Stork
Kleinswartooievaar

77 Marabou Stork
Maraboe

73 Saddle-billed Stork
Saalbekooievaar

112 White Stork
Witooievaar

76 Woolly-necked Stork
Wolnekooievaar

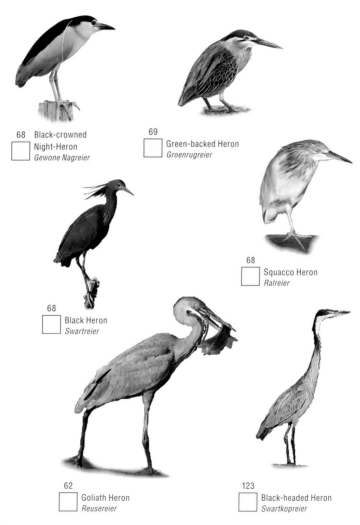

68 Black-crowned
Night-Heron
Gewone Nagreier

69 Green-backed Heron
Groenrugreier

68 Squacco Heron
Ralreier

68 Black Heron
Swartreier

62 Goliath Heron
Reusereier

123 Black-headed Heron
Swartkopreier

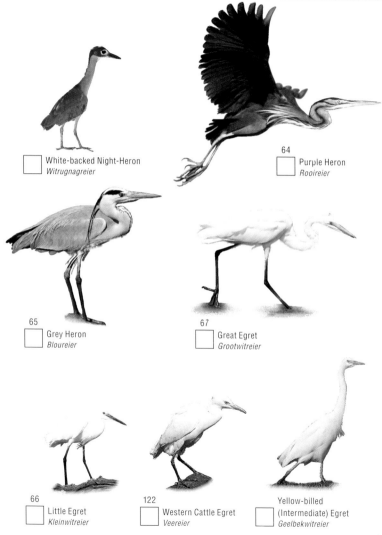

White-backed Night-Heron
Witrugnagreier

64 Purple Heron
Rooireier

65 Grey Heron
Bloureier

67 Great Egret
Grootwitreier

66 Little Egret
Kleinwitreier

122 Western Cattle Egret
Veereier

Yellow-billed
(Intermediate) Egret
Geelbekwitreier

241

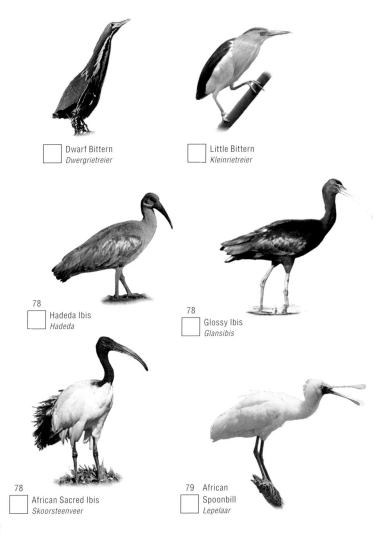

Dwarf Bittern
Dwergrietreier

Little Bittern
Kleinrietreier

78
Hadeda Ibis
Hadeda

78
Glossy Ibis
Glansibis

78
African Sacred Ibis
Skoorsteenveer

79 African
Spoonbill
Lepelaar

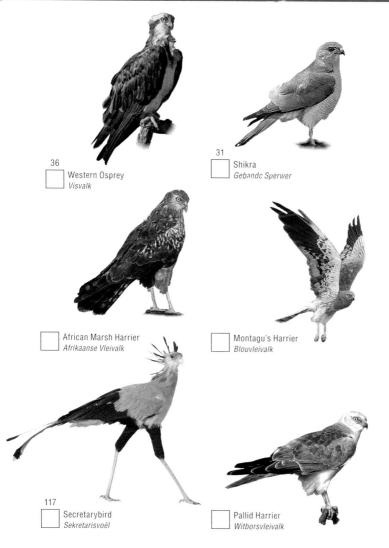

36
Western Osprey
Visvalk

31
Shikra
Gebande Sperwer

African Marsh Harrier
Afrikaanse Vleivalk

Montagu's Harrier
Blouvleivalk

117
Secretarybird
Sekretarisvoël

Pallid Harrier
Witborsvleivalk

243

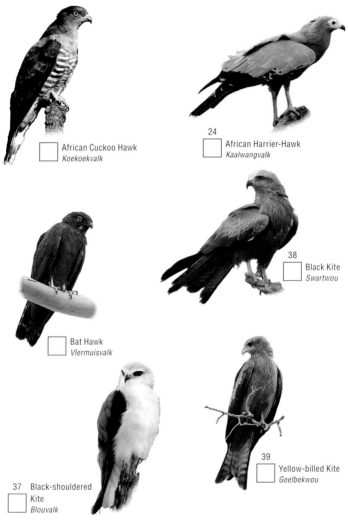

African Cuckoo Hawk
Koekoekvalk

24 African Harrier-Hawk
Kaalwangvalk

Bat Hawk
Vlermuisvalk

38 Black Kite
Swartwou

37 Black-shouldered
Kite
Blouvalk

39 Yellow-billed Kite
Geelbekwou

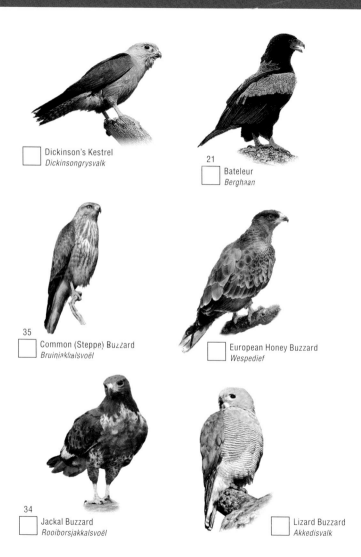

Dickinson's Kestrel
Dickinsongrysvalk

21
Bateleur
Berghaan

35
Common (Steppe) Buzzard
Bruinjakkalsvoël

European Honey Buzzard
Wespedief

34
Jackal Buzzard
Rooiborsjakkalsvoël

Lizard Buzzard
Akkedisvalk

31
☐ African Goshawk
Afrikaanse Sperwer

33
☐ Dark Chanting Goshawk
Donkersingvalk

31
☐ Gabar Goshawk
Witkruissperwer/klein singvalk

18,19 African
☐ Fish Eagle
Visarend

16
☐ African Hawk Eagle
Grootjagarend

☐ Ayres's Hawk Eagle
Kleinjagarend

22 Black-chested
Snake Eagle
Swartborsslangarend

Booted Eagle
Dwergarend

23
Brown Snake Eagle
Bruinslangarend

15
Crowned Eagle
Kroonarend

Lesser Spotted Eagle
Gevlekte Arend

Long-crested Eagle
Langkuifarend

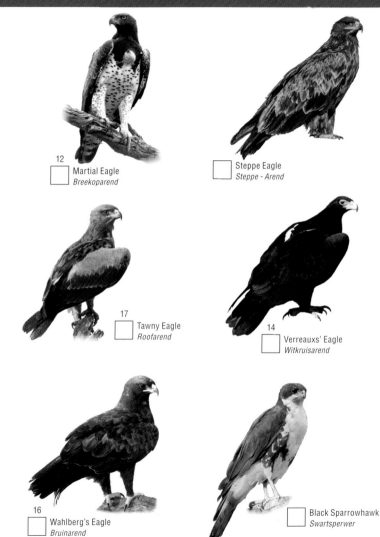

12
Martial Eagle
Breekoparend

Steppe Eagle
Steppe - Arend

17
Tawny Eagle
Roofarend

14
Verreauxs' Eagle
Witkruisarend

16
Wahlberg's Eagle
Bruinarend

Black Sparrowhawk
Swartsperwer

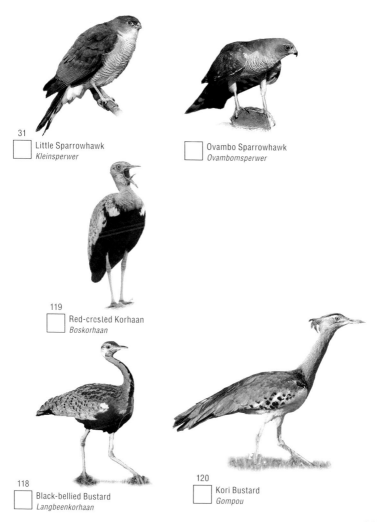

31
Little Sparrowhawk
Kleinsperwer

Ovambo Sparrowhawk
Ovambomsperwer

119
Red-crested Korhaan
Boskorhaan

118
Black-bellied Bustard
Langbeenkorhaan

120
Kori Bustard
Gompou

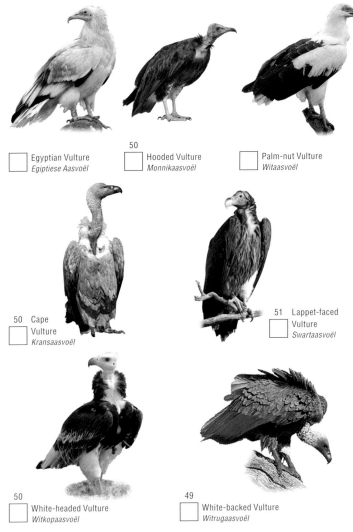

Egyptian Vulture
Egiptiese Aasvoël

50 Hooded Vulture
Monnikaasvoël

Palm-nut Vulture
Witaasvoël

50 Cape Vulture
Kransaasvoël

51 Lappet-faced Vulture
Swartaasvoël

50 White-headed Vulture
Witkopaasvoël

49 White-backed Vulture
Witrugaasvoël

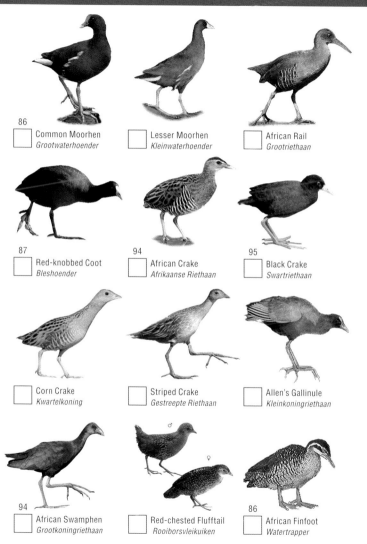

86
Common Moorhen
Grootwaterhoender

Lesser Moorhen
Kleinwaterhoender

African Rail
Grootriethaan

87
Red-knobbed Coot
Bleshoender

94
African Crake
Afrikaanse Riethaan

95
Black Crake
Swartriethaan

Corn Crake
Kwartelkoning

Striped Crake
Gestreepte Riethaan

Allen's Gallinule
Kleinkoningriethaan

94
African Swamphen
Grootkoningriethaan

Red-chested Flufftail
Rooiborsvleikuiken

86
African Finfoot
Watertrapper

251

124 Spotted Thick-knee
Gewone Dikkop

101 Water Thick-knee
Waterdikkop

99 Black-winged Stilt
Rooipootelsie

98 Pied Avocet
Bontelsie

Caspian Plover
Asiatiese Strandkiewiet

90 Common Ringed Plover
Ringnekstrandkiewiet

90 Kittlitz's Plover
Geelborsstrandkiewiet

91 Three-banded Plover
Driebandstrandkiewiet

White-fronted Plover
Vaalstrandkiewiet

92 African Wattled Lapwing
Lelkiewiet

93 Blacksmith Lapwing
Bontkiewiet

125 Crowned Lapwing
Kroonkiewiet

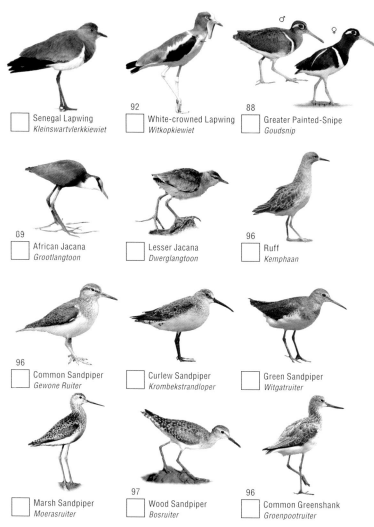

Senegal Lapwing
Kleinswartvlerkkiewiet

92 White-crowned Lapwing
Witkopkiewiet

88 Greater Painted-Snipe
Goudsnip

09 African Jacana
Grootlangtoon

Lesser Jacana
Dwerglangtoon

96 Ruff
Kemphaan

96 Common Sandpiper
Gewone Ruiter

Curlew Sandpiper
Krombekstrandloper

Green Sandpiper
Witgatruiter

Marsh Sandpiper
Moerasruiter

97 Wood Sandpiper
Bosruiter

96 Common Greenshank
Groenpootruiter

253

Little Stint
Kleinstrandloper

94
African Snipe
Afrikaanse Snip

Kurrichane Buttonquail
Bosveldkwarteltjie

125
Bronze-winged Courser
Bronsvlerkdrawwertjie

125
Temminck's Courser
Trekdrawwertjie

Three-banded Courser
Driebanddrawwertjie

Collared Pratincole
Rooivlerksprinkaanvoël

Grey-headed Gull
Gryskopmeeu

African Skimmer
Waterploeër

Whiskered Tern
Witbaardsterretjie

Br
Non-Br
White-winged Tern
Witvlerksterretjie

Eurasian Hobby
Europese Boomvalk

Lesser Kestrel
Kleinrooivalk

28
Rock Kestrel
Kransvalk

Amur Falcon
Oostelike Rooipootvalk

26
Lanner Falcon
Edelvalk

27
Peregrine Falcon
Swerfvalk

Red-footed Falcon
Westelike Rooipootvalk

Sooty Falcon
Roetvalk

Double-banded Sandgrouse
Dubbelbandsandpatrys

255

174 African Green Pigeon
Papegaaiduif

227 Speckled Pigeon
Kransduif

227 African Mourning Dove
Rooioogtortelduif

227 Cape Turtle-Dove
Gewone Tortelduif

227 Emerald-spotted Wood-Dove
Groenvlekduifie

227 Laughing Dove
Rooiborsduifie

226 Namaqua Dove
Namakwaduifie

227 Red-eyed Dove
Grootringduif

Tambourine Dove
Witborsduifie

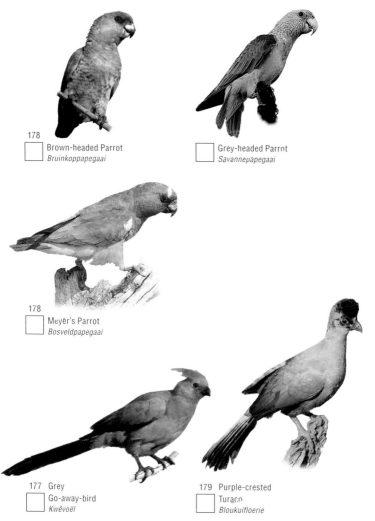

178
Brown-headed Parrot
Bruinkoppapegaai

Grey-headed Parrot
Savannepapegaai

178
Meyer's Parrot
Bosveldpapegaai

177 Grey
Go-away-bird
Kwêvoël

179 Purple-crested
Turaco
Bloukuifloerie

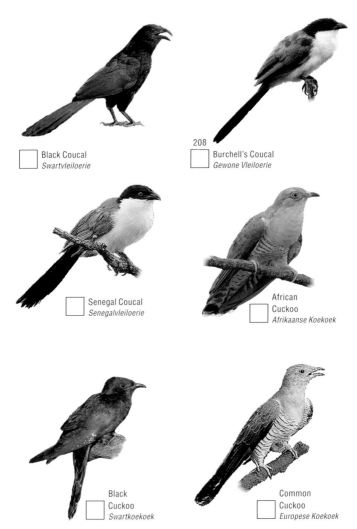

Black Coucal
Swartvleiloerie

208 Burchell's Coucal
Gewone Vleiloerie

Senegal Coucal
Senegalvleiloerie

African Cuckoo
Afrikaanse Koekoek

Black Cuckoo
Swartkoekoek

Common Cuckoo
Europese Koekoek

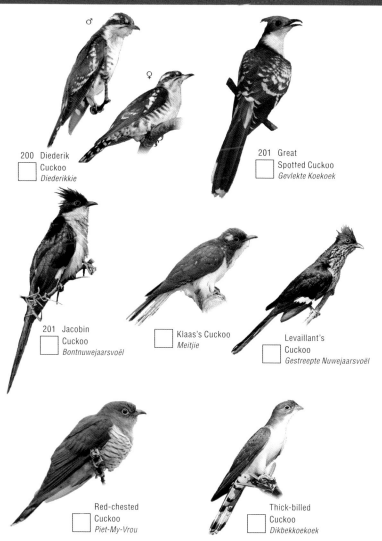

♂

♀

200 Diederik
Cuckoo
Diederikkie

201 Great
Spotted Cuckoo
Gevlekte Koekoek

201 Jacobin
Cuckoo
Bontnuwejaarsvoël

Klaas's Cuckoo
Meitjie

Levaillant's
Cuckoo
Gestreepte Nuwejaarsvoël

Red-chested
Cuckoo
Piet-My-Vrou

Thick-billed
Cuckoo
Dikbekkoekoek

African Grass Owl
Grasuil

44 African Scops Owl
Skopsuil / Witwanguil

47 African Wood Owl
Bosuil

42 Marsh Owl
Vlei-Uil

46 Pel's Fishing Owl
Visuil

42 Southern White-faced Owl
Witwanguil

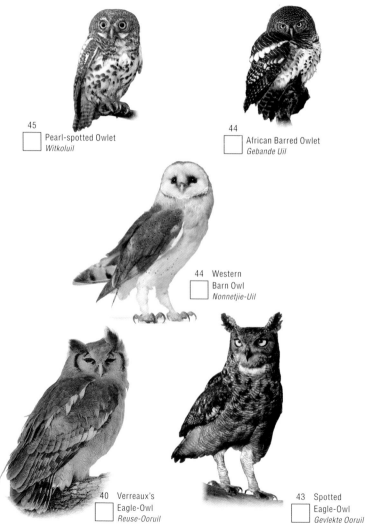

45 Pearl-spotted Owlet
Witkoluil

44 African Barred Owlet
Gebande Uil

44 Western
Barn Owl
Nonnetjie-Uil

40 Verreaux's
Eagle-Owl
Reuse-Ooruil

43 Spotted
Eagle-Owl
Gevlekte Ooruil

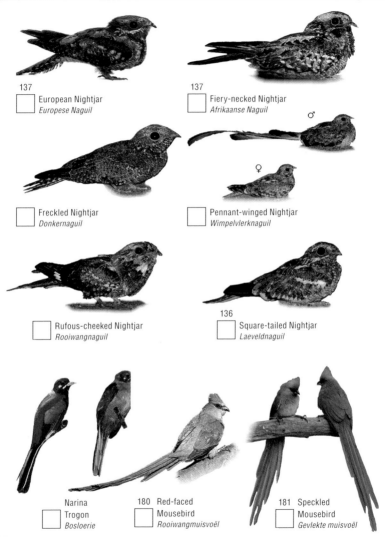

137
☐ European Nightjar
Europese Naguil

137
☐ Fiery-necked Nightjar
Afrikaanse Naguil

☐ Freckled Nightjar
Donkernaguil

☐ Pennant-winged Nightjar
Wimpelvlerknaguil

♂

♀

☐ Rufous-cheeked Nightjar
Rooiwangnaguil

136
☐ Square-tailed Nightjar
Laeveldnaguil

Narina
☐ Trogon
Bosloerie

180 Red-faced
☐ Mousebird
Rooiwangmuisvoël

181 Speckled
☐ Mousebird
Gevlekte muisvoël

☐ African Black Swift
Swartwindswael

☐ African Palm Swift
Palmwindswael

☐ Alpine Swift
Witpenswindswael

☐ Common Swift
Europese Windswael

☐ Horus Swift
Horuswindswael

☐ Little Swift
Kleinwindswael

☐ White-rumped Swift
Witkruiswindswael

☐ Böhm's Spinetail
Witpensstekelstert

☐ Mottled Spinetail
Gevlekte Stekelstert

164 African Pygmy Kingfisher
Dwergvisvanger

107 Malachite Kingfisher
Kuifkopvisvanger

Half-collared Kingfisher
Blouvisvanger

167 Brown-hooded Kingfisher
Bruinkopvisvanger

Grey-headed Kingfisher
Gryskopvisvanger

109 Giant Kingfisher
Reusevisvanger

♂ ♀

108 Pied Kingfisher
Bontvisvanger

♂ ♀

166 Striped Kingfisher
Gestreepte visvanger

165 Woodland Kingfisher
Bosveldvisvanger

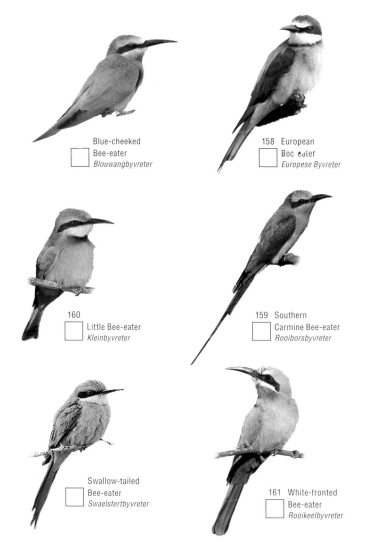

Blue-cheeked
Bee-eater
Blouwangbyvreter

158 European
Boo eater
Europese Byvreter

160
Little Bee-eater
Kleinbyvreter

159 Southern
Carmine Bee-eater
Rooiborsbyvreter

Swallow-tailed
Bee-eater
Swaelstertbyvreter

161 White-fronted
Bee-eater
Rooikeelbyvreter

265

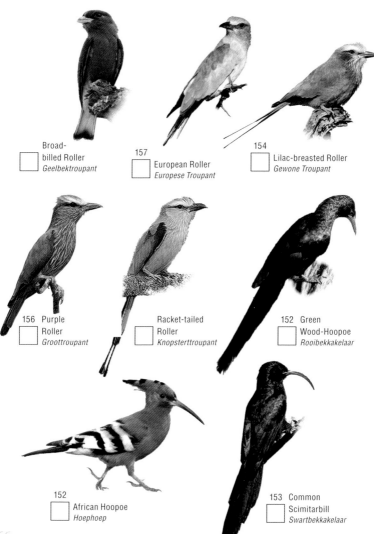

Broad-billed Roller
Geelbektroupant

157 European Roller
Europese Troupant

154 Lilac-breasted Roller
Gewone Troupant

156 Purple Roller
Groottroupant

Racket-tailed Roller
Knopsterttroupant

152 Green Wood-Hoopoe
Rooibekkakelaar

152 African Hoopoe
Hoephoep

153 Common Scimitarbill
Swartbekkakelaar

151 African
Grey Hornbill
Grysneushoringvoël

150 Crowned
Hornbill
Gekroonde Neushoringvoël

149 Southern
Yellow-billed Hornbill
Geelbekneushoringvoël

148 Southern
Red-billed Hornbill
Rooibekneushoringvoël

150 Trumpeter
Hornbill
Gewone Boskraai

114 Southern
Ground-Hornbill
Bromvoël

267

♂ ♀

Bearded
Woodpecker
Baardspeg

145 Bennett's
Woodpecker
Bennettspeg

♂ ♀

146 Cardinal
Woodpecker
Kardinaalspeg

♂ ♀

144
Golden-tailed Woodpecker
Goudstertspeg

♂
♀

Greater Honeyguide
Grootheuningwyser

Lesser Honeyguide
Kleinheuningwyser

Scaly-throated
Honeyguide
Gevlekte Heuningwyser

Brown-backed
Honeybird
Skerpbekheuningvoël

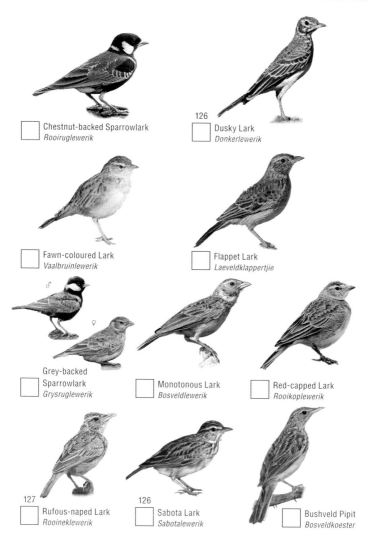

Chestnut-backed Sparrowlark
Rooiruglewerik

126 Dusky Lark
Donkerlewerik

Fawn-coloured Lark
Vaalbruinlewerik

Flappet Lark
Laeveldklappertjie

♂
♀

Grey-backed Sparrowlark
Grysruglewerik

Monotonous Lark
Bosveldlewerik

Red-capped Lark
Rooikoplewerik

127 Rufous-naped Lark
Rooineklewerik

126 Sabota Lark
Sabotalewerik

Bushveld Pipit
Bosveldkoester

269

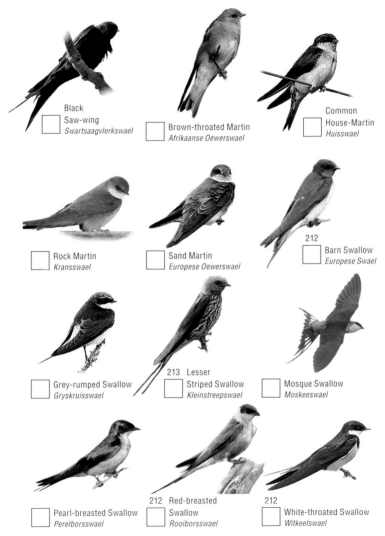

Black
Saw-wing
Swartsaagvlerkswael

Brown-throated Martin
Afrikaanse Oewerswael

Common
House-Martin
Huisswael

Rock Martin
Kransswael

Sand Martin
Europese Oewerswael

212
Barn Swallow
Europese Swael

Grey-rumped Swallow
Gryskruisswael

213 Lesser
Striped Swallow
Kleinstreepswael

Mosque Swallow
Moskeeswael

Pearl-breasted Swallow
Perelborsswael

212 Red-breasted
Swallow
Rooiborsswael

212
White-throated Swallow
Witkeelswael

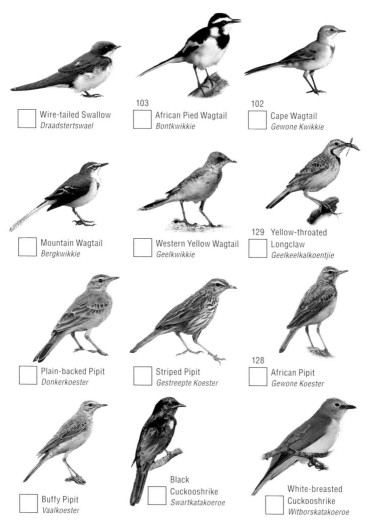

Wire-tailed Swallow
Draadstertswael

103 African Pied Wagtail
Bontkwikkie

102 Cape Wagtail
Gewone Kwikkie

Mountain Wagtail
Bergkwikkie

Western Yellow Wagtail
Geelkwikkie

129 Yellow-throated Longclaw
Geelkeelkalkoentjie

Plain-backed Pipit
Donkerkoester

Striped Pipit
Gestreepte Koester

128 African Pipit
Gewone Koester

Buffy Pipit
Vaalkoester

Black Cuckooshrike
Swartkatakoeroe

White-breasted Cuckooshrike
Witborskatakoeroe

271

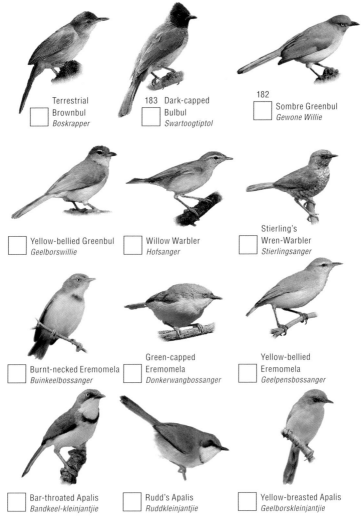

Terrestrial Brownbul
Boskrapper

183 Dark-capped Bulbul
Swartoogtiptol

182 Sombre Greenbul
Gewone Willie

Yellow-bellied Greenbul
Geelborswillie

Willow Warbler
Hofsanger

Stierling's Wren-Warbler
Stierlingsanger

Burnt-necked Eremomela
Buinkeelbossanger

Green-capped Eremomela
Donkerwangbossanger

Yellow-bellied Eremomela
Geelpensbossanger

Bar-throated Apalis
Bandkeel-kleinjantjie

Rudd's Apalis
Ruddkleinjantjie

Yellow-breasted Apalis
Geelborskleinjantjie

Croaking Cisticola
Groot Tinktinkie

Desert Cisticola
Woestynklopkloppie

Lazy Cisticola
Luitinktinkie

194

Rattling Cisticola
Bosveldtinktinkie

Red-faced Cisticola
Rooiwangtinktinkie

Rufous-winged Cisticola
Swartrugtinktinkie

Zitting Cisticola
Landeryklopkloppie

Green-backed
Camaroptera
Groenrugkwekwevoël

Grey-backed
Camaroptera
Grysrugkwekwevoël

Neddicky
Neddikkie

Tawny-flanked Prinia
Bruinsylangstertjie

194

Long-billed Crombec
Bosveldstompstert

273

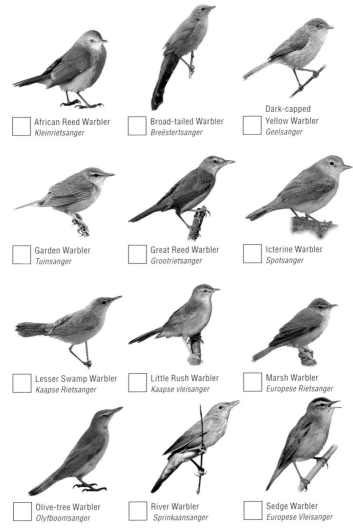

African Reed Warbler
Kleinrietsanger

Broad-tailed Warbler
Breëstertsanger

Dark-capped
Yellow Warbler
Geelsanger

Garden Warbler
Tuinsanger

Great Reed Warbler
Grootrietsanger

Icterine Warbler
Spotsanger

Lesser Swamp Warbler
Kaapse Rietsanger

Little Rush Warbler
Kaapse vleisanger

Marsh Warbler
Europese Rietsanger

Olive-tree Warbler
Olyfboomsanger

River Warbler
Sprinkaansanger

Sedge Warbler
Europese Vleisanger

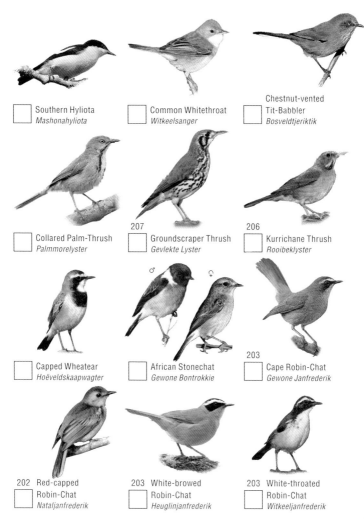

☐ Southern Hyliota
Mashonahyliota

☐ Common Whitethroat
Witkeelsanger

Chestnut-vented
☐ Tit-Babbler
Bosveldtjeriktik

207
☐ Collared Palm-Thrush
Palmmorelyster

☐ Groundscraper Thrush
Gevlekte Lyster

206
☐ Kurrichane Thrush
Rooibeklyster

☐ Capped Wheatear
Hoëveldskaapwagter

♂ ♀
☐ African Stonechat
Gewone Bontrokkie

203
☐ Cape Robin-Chat
Gewone Janfrederik

202 Red-capped
☐ Robin-Chat
Nataljanfrederik

203 White-browed
☐ Robin-Chat
Heuglinjanfrederik

203 White-throated
☐ Robin-Chat
Witkeeljanfrederik

275

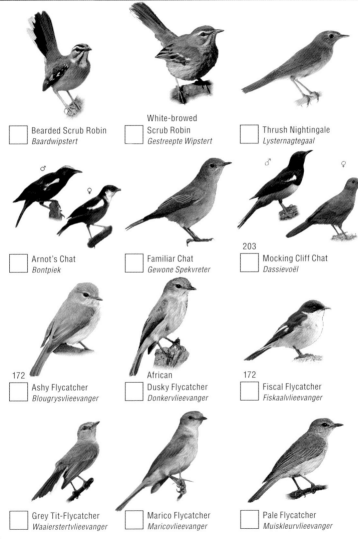

Bearded Scrub Robin
Baardwipstert

White-browed
Scrub Robin
Gestreepte Wipstert

Thrush Nightingale
Lysternagtegaal

Arnot's Chat
Bontpiek

Familiar Chat
Gewone Spekvreter

203
Mocking Cliff Chat
Dassievoël

172
Ashy Flycatcher
Blougrysvlieevanger

African
Dusky Flycatcher
Donkervlieevanger

172
Fiscal Flycatcher
Fiskaalvlieevanger

Grey Tit-Flycatcher
Waaierstertvlieevanger

Marico Flycatcher
Maricovlieevanger

Pale Flycatcher
Muiskleurvlieevanger

Southern Black Flycatcher
Swartvlieevanger

173 Spotted Flycatcher
Europese Vlieevanger

Cape Batis
Kaapse Bosbontrokkie

195 Chinspot Batis
Witliesbosbontrokkie

Black-throated Wattle-eye
Beloogbosbontrokkie

173 African Paradise Flycatcher
Paradysvlieevanger

Blue-mantled Crested-Flycatcher
Bloukuifvlieevanger

204 Arrow-marked Babbler
Pylvlekkatlagter

143 Crested Barbet
Kuifkophoutkapper

142 Acacia Pied Barbet
Bonthoutkapper

141 Black-collared Barbet
Rooihoutkapper

Yellow-fronted Tinkerbird
Geelblestinker

277

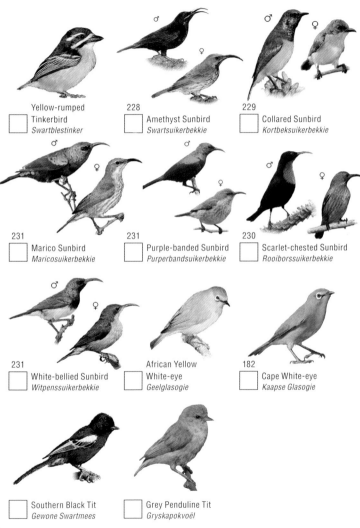

Yellow-rumped
Tinkerbird
Swartblestinker

228
Amethyst Sunbird
Swartsuikerbekkie

229
Collared Sunbird
Kortbeksuikerbekkie

231
Marico Sunbird
Maricosuikerbekkie

231
Purple-banded Sunbird
Purperbandsuikerbekkie

230
Scarlet-chested Sunbird
Rooiborssuikerbekkie

231
White-bellied Sunbird
Witpenssuikerbekkie

African Yellow
White-eye
Geelglasogie

182
Cape White-eye
Kaapse Glasogie

Southern Black Tit
Gewone Swartmees

Grey Penduline Tit
Gryskapokvoël

278

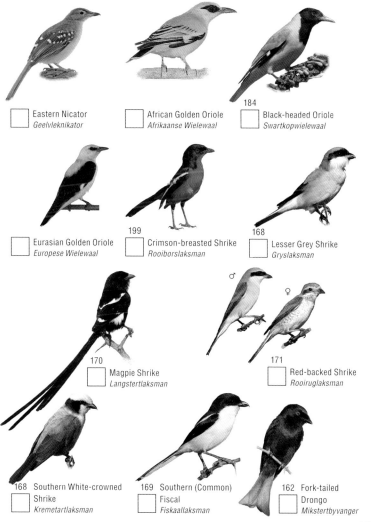

Eastern Nicator
Geelvleknikator

African Golden Oriole
Afrikaanse Wielewaal

184 Black-headed Oriole
Swartkopwielewaal

Eurasian Golden Oriole
Europese Wielewaal

199 Crimson-breasted Shrike
Rooiborslaksman

168 Lesser Grey Shrike
Gryslaksman

170 Magpie Shrike
Langstertlaksman

171 Red-backed Shrike
Rooiruglaksman

168 Southern White-crowned Shrike
Kremetartlaksman

169 Southern (Common) Fiscal
Fiskaallaksman

162 Fork-tailed Drongo
Mikstertbyvanger

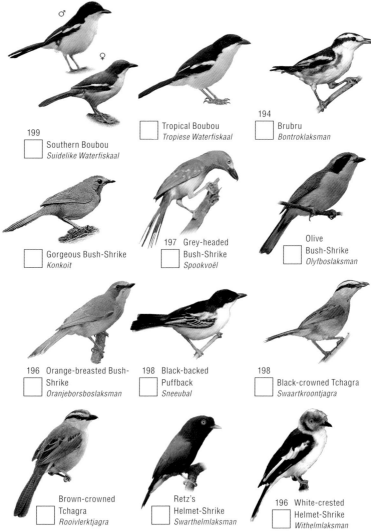

♂

♀

199
Southern Boubou
Suidelike Waterfiskaal

Tropical Boubou
Tropiese Waterfiskaal

194
Brubru
Bontroklaksman

Gorgeous Bush-Shrike
Konkoit

197 Grey-headed
Bush-Shrike
Spookvoël

Olive
Bush-Shrike
Olyfboslaksman

196 Orange-breasted Bush-
Shrike
Oranjeborsboslaksman

198 Black-backed
Puffback
Sneeubal

198
Black-crowned Tchagra
Swaartkroontjagra

Brown-crowned
Tchagra
Rooivlerktjagra

Retz's
Helmet-Shrike
Swarthelmlaksman

196 White-crested
Helmet-Shrike
Withelmlaksman

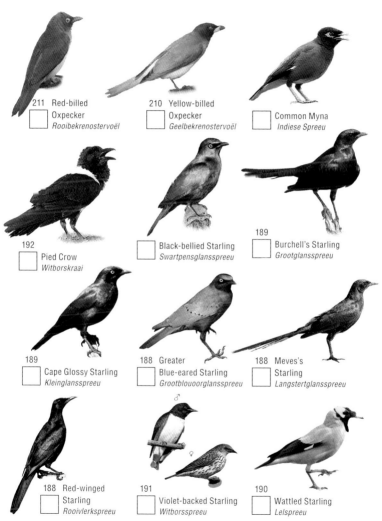

211 Red-billed Oxpecker
Rooibekrenostervoël

210 Yellow-billed Oxpecker
Geelbekrenostervoël

Common Myna
Indiese Spreeu

192 Pied Crow
Witborskraai

Black-bellied Starling
Swartpensglansspreeu

189 Burchell's Starling
Grootglansspreeu

189 Cape Glossy Starling
Kleinglansspreeu

188 Greater Blue-eared Starling
Grootblouoorglansspreeu

188 Meves's Starling
Langstertglansspreeu

188 Red-winged Starling
Rooivlerkspreeu

191 Violet-backed Starling
Witborsspreeu

190 Wattled Starling
Lelspreeu

281

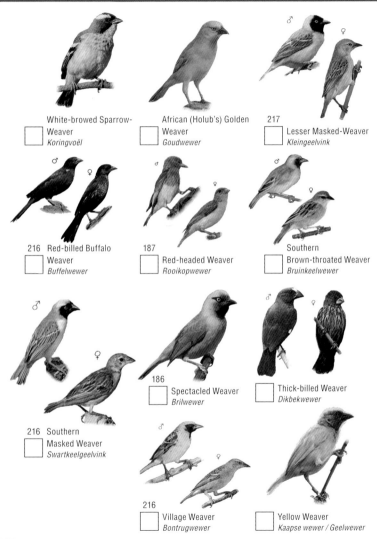

White-browed Sparrow-Weaver
Koringvoël

African (Holub's) Golden Weaver
Goudwewer

217
Lesser Masked-Weaver
Kleingeelvink

216 Red-billed Buffalo Weaver
Buffelwewer

187
Red-headed Weaver
Rooikopwewer

Southern Brown-throated Weaver
Bruinkeelwewer

216 Southern Masked Weaver
Swartkeelgeelvink

186
Spectacled Weaver
Brilwewer

Thick-billed Weaver
Dikbekwewer

216
Village Weaver
Bontrugwewer

Yellow Weaver
Kaapse wewer / Geelwewer

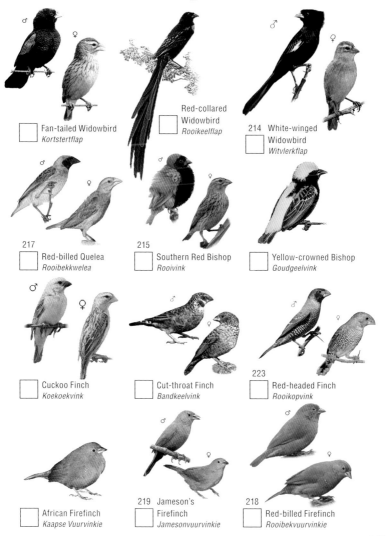

Fan-tailed Widowbird
Kortstertflap

Red-collared Widowbird
Rooikeelflap

214 White-winged Widowbird
Witvlerkflap

217 Red-billed Quelea
Rooibekkwelea

215 Southern Red Bishop
Rooivink

Yellow-crowned Bishop
Goudgeelvink

Cuckoo Finch
Koekoekvink

Cut-throat Finch
Bandkeelvink

223 Red-headed Finch
Rooikopvink

African Firefinch
Kaapse Vuurvinkie

219 Jameson's Firefinch
Jamesonvuurvinkie

218 Red-billed Firefinch
Rooibekvuurvinkie

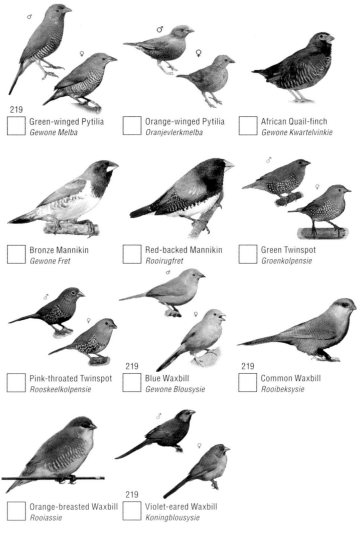

219
☐ Green-winged Pytilia
Gewone Melba

☐ Orange-winged Pytilia
Oranjevlerkmelba

☐ African Quail-finch
Gewone Kwartelvinkie

☐ Bronze Mannikin
Gewone Fret

☐ Red-backed Mannikin
Rooirugfret

☐ Green Twinspot
Groenkolpensie

☐ Pink-throated Twinspot
Rooskeelkolpensie

219
☐ Blue Waxbill
Gewone Blousysie

219
☐ Common Waxbill
Rooibeksysie

☐ Orange-breasted Waxbill
Rooiassie

219
☐ Violet-eared Waxbill
Koningblousysie

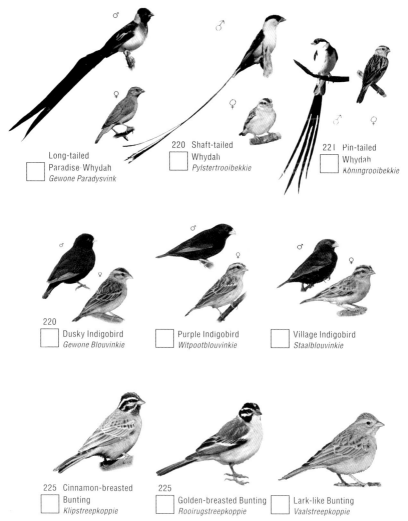

♂ ♀

Long-tailed
Paradise Whydah
Gewone Paradysvink

220 Shaft-tailed
Whydah
Pylstertrooibekkie

221 Pin-tailed
Whydah
Koningrooibekkie

220
Dusky Indigobird
Gewone Blouvinkie

Purple Indigobird
Witpootblouvinkie

Village Indigobird
Staalblouvinkie

225 Cinnamon-breasted
Bunting
Klipstreepkoppie

225
Golden-breasted Bunting
Rooirugstreepkoppie

Lark-like Bunting
Vaalstreepkoppie

285

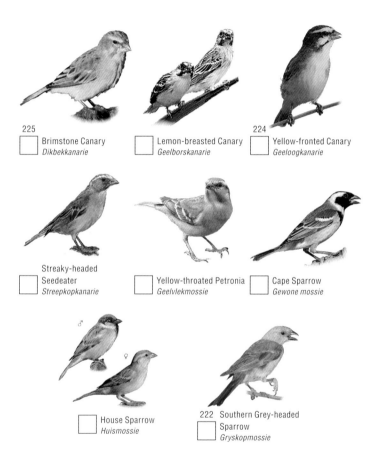

225
Brimstone Canary
Dikbekkanarie

Lemon-breasted Canary
Geelborskanarie

224
Yellow-fronted Canary
Geeloogkanarie

Streaky-headed
Seedeater
Streepkopkanarie

Yellow-throated Petronia
Geelvlekmossie

Cape Sparrow
Gewone mossie

House Sparrow
Huismossie

222 Southern Grey-headed
Sparrow
Gryskopmossie

Cape Sparrow

Helmeted Guineafowl

INDEX

A

B

C

D

E

F

G

H

M

N

O

P

Q

R

S

T

V